IS-302: Modular Emergency Radiological Response Transportation Training

By

Fema

INTRODUCTION

The reliance upon, and use of, radioactive material in agriculture, industry, and medicine continues to increase. As the manufacture, use, and disposal of radioactive material has increased, so has the need to transport it. Consequently, the potential for you as a responder to encounter an incident involving some type of radioactive material has increased. Having knowledge of radiological hazards, and the terminology used to describe them, will increase your ability to quickly recognize, safely respond, and accurately relay information during an incident involving radioactive material.

PURPOSE

Upon completion of this module, you will have a better understanding of the basic structure of an atom and the fundamentals of radiation.

MODULE OBJECTIVES

Upon completion of this module, you will be able to:

1. Identify the basic components of an atom.
2. Define ionizing radiation, radioactivity, radioactive material, and radioactive contamination.
3. Distinguish between radiation and contamination.
4. Identify some commonly transported sources of radioactive material.

notes

BACKGROUND

Radiation is all around us and has been present since the birth of this planet. Today, both man-made and natural radioactive material are part of our daily lives. We use radioactive material for beneficial purposes, such as generating electricity and diagnosing and treating medical conditions. Radiation is used in many ways to improve our health and the quality of our lives.

In 1895, while working in his laboratory, Wilhelm Roentgen discovered a previously unknown phenomenon: rays that could penetrate solid objects. Roentgen called these rays "X-rays." The figure at right shows Roentgen's wife's left hand - the first known X-ray. The practical uses of X-rays were quickly recognized and, within a few months, a medical X-ray picture was used to locate shotgun pellets in a man's hand.

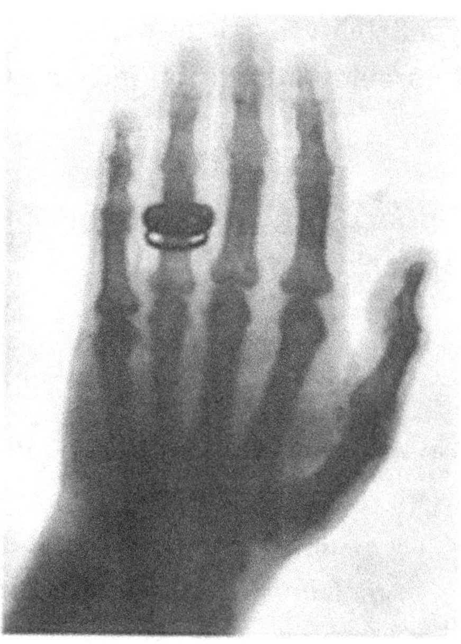

In 1896, Henri Becquerel reported observing a similar radiological phenomenon caused by uranium ore. Later that year, Pierre and Marie Curie identified the source of the radiation as a small concentration of radium, a radioactive material, in the ore.

These discoveries set the stage for using radiation in medicine, industry, and research. Since that time, scientist have developed a detailed understanding of the hazards and benefits of radiation. In fact, scientists understand radiological hazards better than hazards associated with most other physical and chemical agents.

M E R R T T
Radiological Basics

BASIC RADIOLOGICAL CONCEPTS

Atomic Structure

All matter is made up of atoms. Atoms are invisible to the naked eye. The three basic components of the atom are protons, neutrons, and electrons. The central portion of the atom is the nucleus. The nucleus contains protons and neutrons, which are very close to each other. Electrons orbit the nucleus.

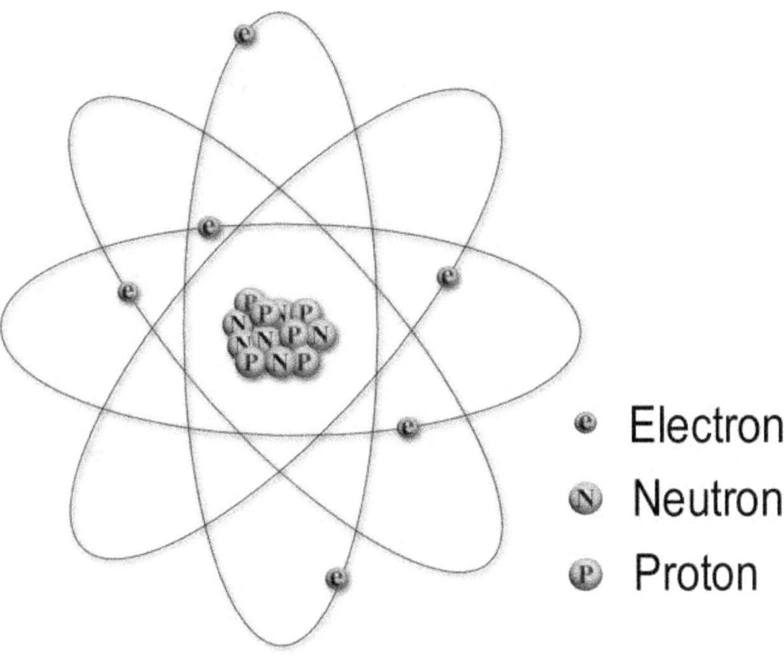

Protons
- Are located in the atom's nucleus
- Have a positive electrical charge
- Determine the element's identity

Neutrons
- Are located in the atom's nucleus
- Have a neutral electrical charge
- Determine the nuclear properties of the atom

Electrons
- Orbit the nucleus
- Have a negative electrical charge
- Determine the chemical properties of an atom

notes

Atoms of a particular element will the same number of protons but may have a different number of neutrons. These variants are called isotopes. Isotopes of the same element have the same chemical properties, regardless of the number of neutrons. The nuclear properties of isotopes, however, can be quite different. For example, the illustration below shows three isotopes of hydrogen. All three isotopes have the same chemical properties; however, tritium is a radioactive isotope or radioisotope.

Isotopes of Hydrogen

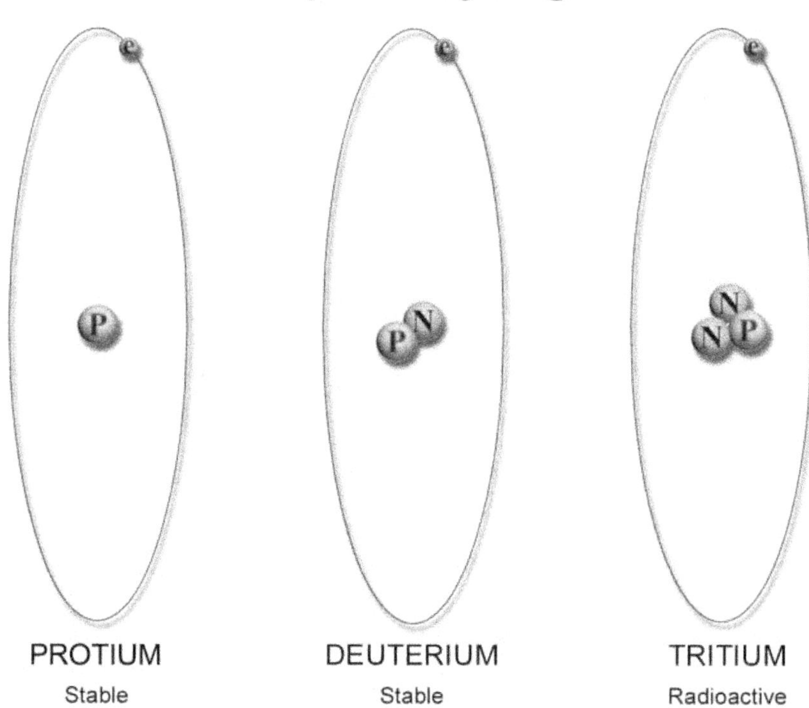

Stable and Unstable Atoms

Only certain combinations of neutrons and protons result in stable atoms.

- If there are too many or too few neutrons for a given number of protons, the resulting nucleus will have too much energy. This atom will not be stable.
- An unstable atom will try to become stable by giving off excess energy in the form of radiation (particles or waves). Unstable atoms are also known as radioactive atoms.

M E R R T T
Radiological Basics

IONIZING RADIATION

As an emergency responder, you may already be familiar with some radiation terminology and with some radiological concepts. When most people think of radiation, they think of the type we are talking about in this course—the type that comes from atoms. There are, however, many different kinds of radiation. Visible light, heat, radio waves, and microwaves are all examples of radiation that, as a group, are referred to as electromagnetic radiation. The graphic below shows the electromagnetic spectrum. As the graphic illustrates, radiation such as radio waves and microwaves are much lower in energy than X-rays or cosmic rays. These lower energy radiations are referred to as non-ionizing radiation. Higher energy radiation like X-rays or cosmic rays are referred to as ionizing radiation.

The Electromagnetic Spectrum

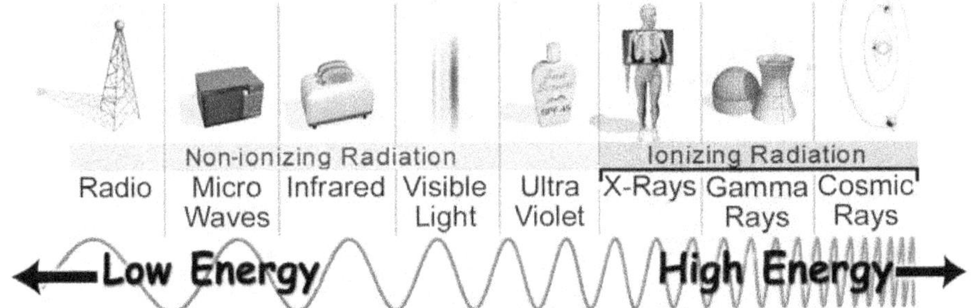

Ionizing radiation has enough energy to remove electrons from atoms. The process of removing electrons from atoms is called ionization. Ionizing radiation's ability to remove electrons from atoms is what makes it potentially hazardous. In this course, when we speak of radiation, we're talking about ionizing radiation. The ionization process is illustrated in the graphic below:

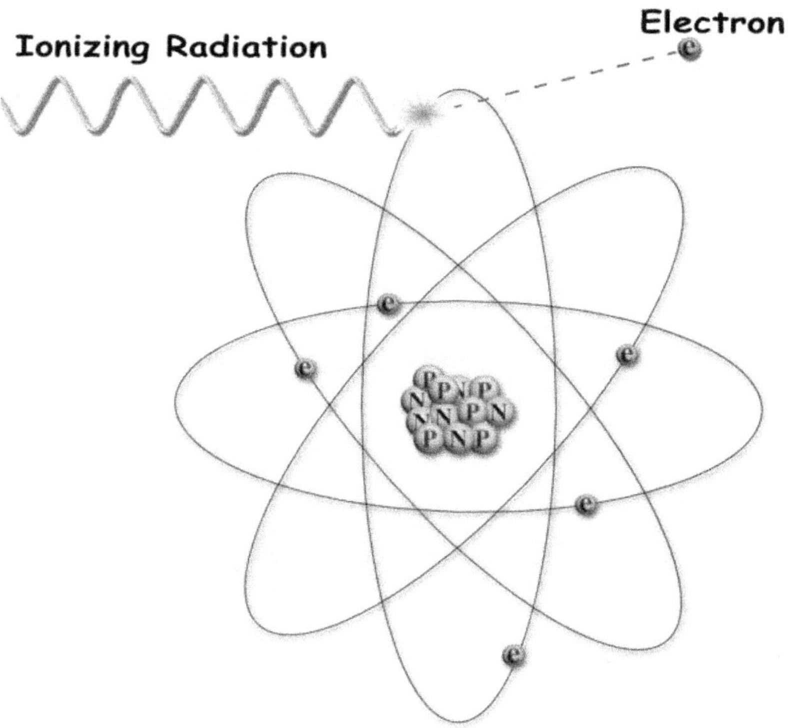

Radioactive Material and Radioactivity

Radioactive material is any material that spontaneously emits ionizing radiation. The process of an unstable atom emitting radiation is called radioactivity. Radioactive atoms can be generated through nuclear processes but they also exist naturally in material such as uranium ore, thorium rock, and some forms of potassium. When a radioactive atom goes through the process of radioactivity, also called radioactive decay, it will change to another type of atom. In fact, a radioactive atom may change from one element to another element during the decay process. For example, the element uranium will eventually change through radioactive decay to lead. This stabilizing process may take from a fraction of a second to billions of years, depending on the isotope.

The rate of radioactive decay is unique to each type of radioactive atom and is measured in half-lives, the time it takes for half of the radioactive atoms in a sample to decay to another form. Different radioactive materials have different half-lives. For example, some radioactive pharmaceutical products (called radiopharmaceuticals) have half-lives that range from a few hours to a few months. It is important to note that radioactivity, regardless of the material, is constantly decreasing. After seven half-lives, the material will be at <1% of its original activity. The table below lists some common radioisotopes and their approximate half-life.

Radioisotope	Half-life
Nitrogen-16	7 seconds
Technetium-99m	6 hours
Thallium-201	73 hours
Cobalt-60	5 years
Cesium-137	30 years
Americium-247	432 years
Uranium-238	4.5 billion years

Radioactive Contamination

Any material that spontaneously emits ionizing radiation is a radioactive material. If radioactive material is in a place where we don't want it (e.g., deposited on the surfaces of or inside structures, areas, objects, or people) it is called radioactive contamination. The photo below illustrates contamination by showing a radiopharmaceutical package broken open with the contents spilled on the ground.

When radioactive material is properly used and controlled, there are many beneficial applications. Most smoke detectors, for instance, use radioactive material, as do certain medical diagnostic tools and treatment procedures. It is only when radioactive material is where it is not wanted (e.g., on the ground, in water, or on you) that we refer to it as contamination.

RADIATION VERSUS CONTAMINATION

One of the most important concepts for the responder to understand is the difference between radiation and contamination. Radiation is energy emitted by radioactive material (as illustrated by arrows). Contamination is radioactive material in a location where it is not wanted.

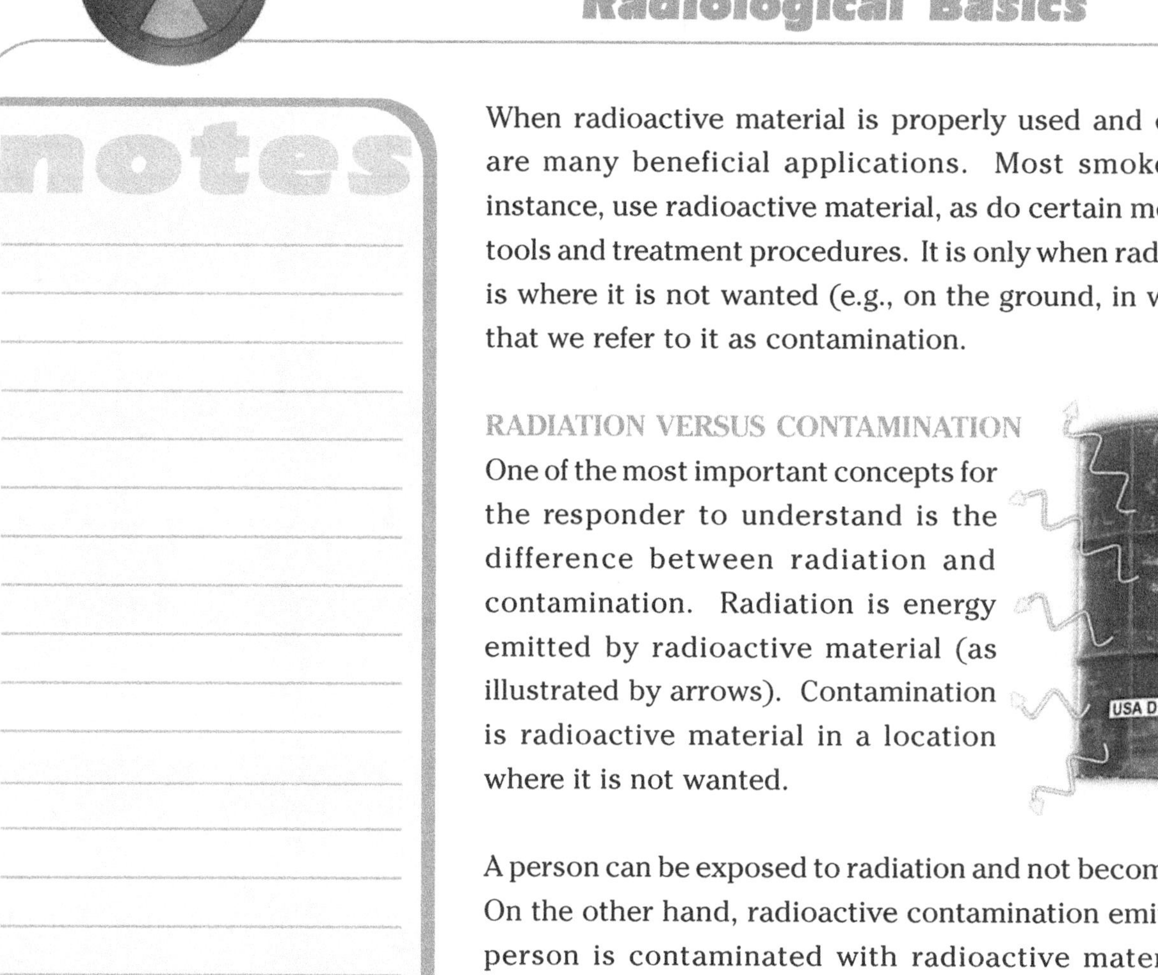

A person can be exposed to radiation and not become contaminated. On the other hand, radioactive contamination emits radiation. If a person is contaminated with radioactive material, the person continues to be exposed to radiation until the contamination is removed.

Put another way, radiation exposure is like being in front of a heat lamp. When the lamp is on, you can feel the heat. When you turn the lamp off, the heat is no longer felt. The heat is similar to exposure. The source of the energy is not in or on you and the exposure stops when you turn off the lamp. Contamination of a person happens when the source of radiation (radioactive material) gets on or in the person. You can be exposed to radiation and not be contaminated. However, if you become contaminated, you will continue to be exposed to radiation until the contamination is removed.

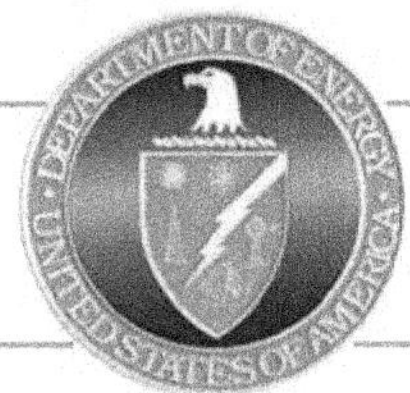

M E R R T T
Radiological Basics

Exposure to Radioactive Material

If you encounter radioactive material at an incident scene, you may be exposed to radiation. Even with the tightest package and the best protection, low levels of radiation can pass through the package. This radiation is at a level that is (based on numerous scientific studies by a variety of industry, scientific, and government organizations) considered safe for people working near the packages. If the packages are intact, you should not expect unsafe exposure.

You should remember that we are exposed to radiation every day from common sources such as cosmic rays, X-rays, and even the bricks used to make buildings. Being exposed to radiation at these controlled levels is a very low hazard and should not prevent you from taking normal emergency actions. Exposure to radiation alone will not contaminate you.

Radioactive Contamination Types

A more serious concern is the possibility of radioactive contamination. The probability of radioactive material being released during an incident is extremely low. If radioactive material is released (as illustrated in the photo below), it is possible for responders, victims, and onlookers to become contaminated. This is especially true where the material is in the form of a liquid or powder.

There are two basic types of radioactive contamination: external or internal. Radioactive contamination is serious because as long as the material is on you, your clothing, or inside your body, you are still being exposed. While a short exposure to these materials may be safe, prolonged or very close exposure may not be.

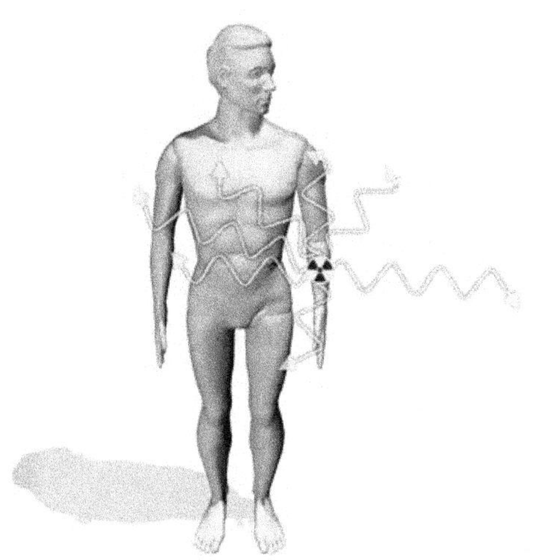

External Contamination

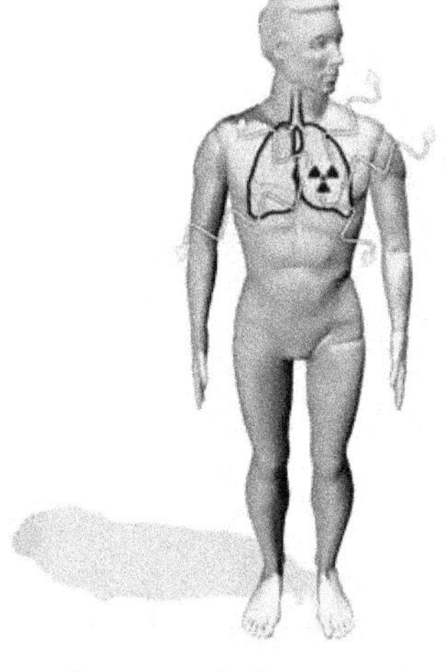

Internal Contamination

A special concern is the possibility of internal contamination. This happens when a radioactive material—usually a liquid, powder, or gas—is accidentally ingested or inhaled or otherwise gets inside the body. Once inside the body, it can be difficult to remove.

Radioactive material that might not be very dangerous outside the body may be dangerous if allowed to enter the body. For this reason, throughout this training, we will emphasize the use of personal protective equipment (PPE) and the importance of not eating, drinking, smoking, or chewing while on the scene of a radioactive material incident.

Another concern is that people who are contaminated externally may contaminate others, either directly or by secondary contamination. Secondary contamination occurs when a contaminated person or object touches something, that is then touched by another, who then becomes contaminated.

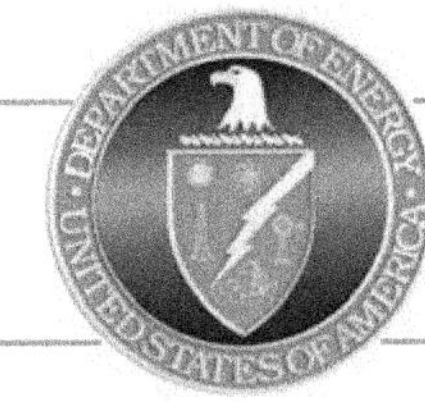

The following example describes how contamination is often spread. Imagine chalk on a blackboard as being radioactive material. If the chalk dust is transferred to your hands, you are considered contaminated. From your hand, the chalk dust can then be transferred to your shirt. The transfer of contamination from your hands to your shirt is an example of secondary or cross contamination.

COMMON SOURCES OF RADIOACTIVE MATERIAL

Everything is exposed to background ionizing radiation from naturally occurring sources. Radiation comes from many sources: the earth's crust, water, the air, and cosmic rays and particles. A portion of the world's population is also exposed to man-made sources of radiation through medical procedures that use radioactive material and X-rays. Even our bodies contain naturally occurring radioactive material.

What does radioactive material look like? As with other hazardous material, radioactive material exists in all physical forms–solids, liquids, and gases. The following are some commonly used and transported radioactive materials that you may be likely to encounter as a first responder.

M E R R T T
Radiological Basics

Radiopharmaceuticals - are radioactive drugs used for medical diagnoses and in radiation therapy. Radiopharmaceuticals are the most commonly transported radioactive material in the U.S. Most radiopharmaceuticals have very short half-lives and are typically transported by air and express delivery services. These materials can be in liquid, gas, powdered, or solid form.

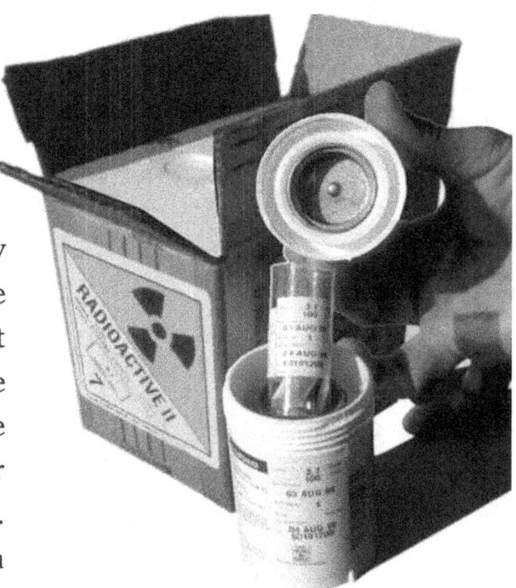

Consumer products - smoke detectors are an example of a commonly transported consumer product. The amount of radioactivity in the household smoke detector falls below regulatory limits and therefore these materials will not be marked or labeled as "radioactive material" during transport.

Industrial sources - are specially designed and sealed sources of radiation used in construction and other industrial applications to check welds and metal for flaws, to check concrete and asphalt, and to test the density of soil. Soil density gauges are one example of a commonly transported industrial source. They usually contain a cesium-137 and/or americium-241:beryllium source. These types of gauges do not typically contain life-endangering amounts of radioactive material. Radiography sources, on the other hand, often contain a very high level source (commonly iridium-192 or cobalt-60) that could pose a high exposure risk if the source were outside of its packaging. When these sources are transported, they are shipped in very robust shipping packages.

M E R R T T
Radiological Basics

Pictured below from top to bottom are: a soil density gauge sitting outside of its shipping/carrying case; a radiography camera outside its shipping/carrying case; and an example of a radiography source (commonly referred to as a "pigtail"). The pigtail is secured inside the radiography camera.

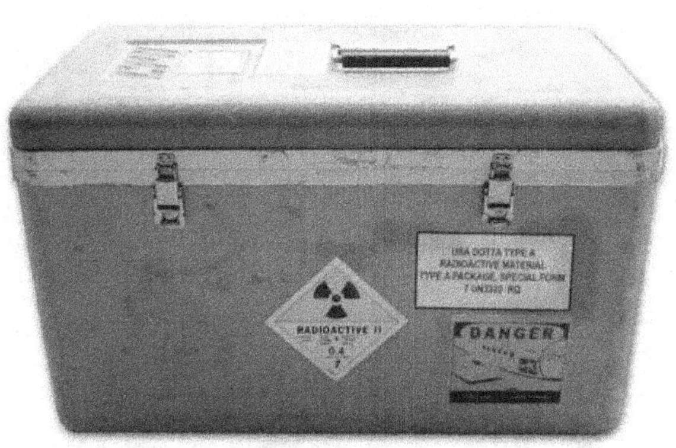

Radiography camera and overpack

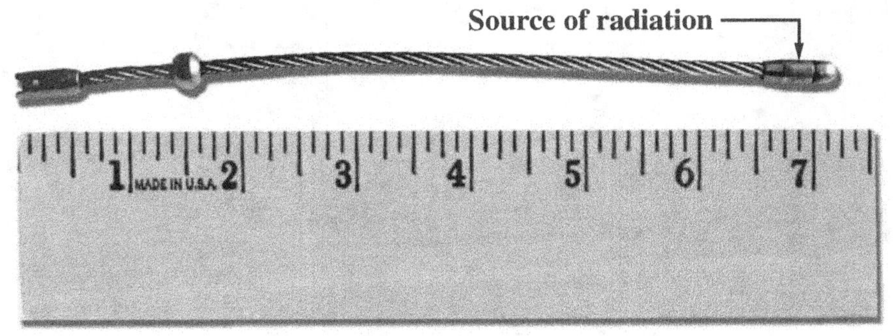

Nuclear fuels - nuclear fuel may be either new fuel being transported to a nuclear power station or spent (used) fuel being transported for reprocessing, storage, or disposal. These materials are solid in form and transported in specially designed packages called shipping casks. Pictured below is a spent fuel shipping cask being surveyed by radiological control personnel.

Radioactive waste - waste material comes from nuclear power generating facilities, nuclear processing plants, research institutions, medical facilities, or other locations. Radioactive waste is commonly transported by highway and rail. Pictured below are 55-gallon drums of radioactive waste (typically containing items such as contaminated protective clothing, rags, etc.) and, on the following page, a railcar loaded with contaminated soil from cleanup operations at a DOE facility.

M E R R T T
Radiological Basics

Radioactive material is one of the most highly regulated hazardous materials transported. The U.S. Department of Transportation regulates domestic shipments of radioactive material. Both the U.S. Nuclear Regulatory Commission and the U.S. Environmental Protection Agency have a role in assisting with development of the hazardous material shipping regulations. The philosophy for managing the transport of radioactive material is highly proactive. Radioactive material has been moved across this country for more than 50 years and, to date, there has never been a death or injury resulting from exposure to this material during transport.

Check Your *Understanding*

1. Atoms are made up of _______, _______, and _______.

2. The process of removing _______ from atoms is called ionization.

3. Radioactive material is any material that spontaneously emits _______ _______.

4. The process of an unstable atom emitting radiation is called _______.

5. Radioactive material in an unwanted location is called _______.

6. _______ can pass through the body; _______ can be deposited in or on the surface of the body.

7. One commonly transported source of radioactive material is (pick one):
   a) Radio waves
   b) Visible light
   c) Radiopharmaceuticals
   d) Microwaves

ANSWERS

1. protons
   neutrons
   electrons
2. electrons
3. ionizing
   radiation
4. radioactivity
5. contamination
6. radiation
   contamination
7. c

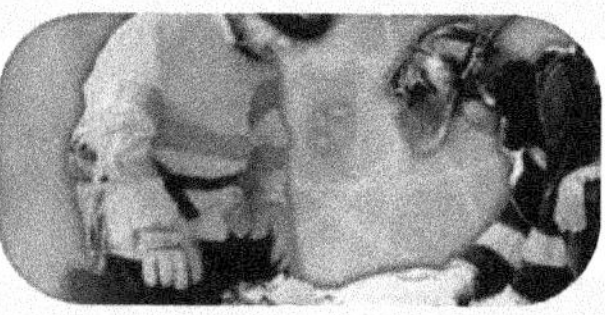

INTRODUCTION

In this module you will learn about the potential health effects of ionizing radiation, acute and chronic radiation exposure, and ways that radioactive material can enter the body. You will learn that the potential for you to receive a significant or damaging amount of radiation during an emergency response situation is extremely low.

PURPOSE

The purpose of this module is to increase your understanding of how ionizing radiation affects the human body. This knowledge will help you, as a responder, function with confidence during incidents that involve radioactive material.

MODULE OBJECTIVES

Upon completion of this module, you will be able to:

1. Define acute and chronic radiation doses.

2. Identify ways that radioactive material can enter the body.

3. Identify the potential health effects of radiation exposure.

RADIATION: Dose and Dose Rate

We live with radiation every day. We receive radiation exposures from cosmic rays, from outer space, from radon gas, and from other naturally radioactive elements in the earth. This is called natural background radiation. It includes the radiation we get from plants, animals, and from the natural sources within our own bodies.

We are also exposed to man-made sources of radiation, including medical and dental treatments, television sets and emission from coal-fired power plants. Generally, radiation exposures from man-made sources are only a fraction of those received from natural sources.

Radiation dose is the amount of radiation energy deposited in the body. Radiation dose rate is a measure of the rate at which radiation energy is deposited in the body. Radiation dose rate is measured in terms of exposure per unit of time. This is like the speedometer and odometer in your car. The speedometer measures your rate of speed—like dose rate. And, the odometer measures the total distance traveled—like total dose received.

Radiation dose is usually measured in terms of millirem and radiation dose rate is usually measured in terms of millirem per hour. In the United States, the annual average radiation dose per person from all sources is about 360 millirem; however, it isn't uncommon for any of us to receive far more than that in a given year (largely due to medical procedures we may have done). As an example, workers at nuclear facilities are allowed up to 5,000 millirem of radiation exposure each year.

Radiation Risk

Exposure to radiation may cause detrimental effects. Understanding the risks will allow you to evaluate risks and benefits associated with a potential exposure. Understanding the risks will also help you to minimize those risks.

We know that radiation has the ability to damage living cells, causing modification of the cell or cell death. Most organs and tissues of the body are not affected by the loss of even considerable numbers of cells. However, if the number lost is large enough, there will be

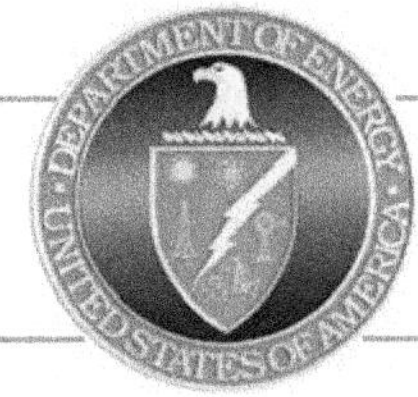

observable harm to organs which may lead to outward observable effects and in some cases death. Such harm occurs in individuals who are exposed to large radiation doses in a short period of time. Cells that are damaged but do not die as a result of radiation exposure often repair the damage such that there are no adverse health consequences. If the damage to the cell is not repaired, the resulting modification may be transmitted to future cells and may eventually lead to cancer. These effects may take years to manifest.

BIOLOGICAL EFFECTS OF IONIZING RADIATION

Scientists began to collect and analyze information about the biological effects of ionizing radiation shortly after its discovery. Since that time, scientists have continued studies of radiation effects on cells, plants, animals, and humans. Although we don't have any concrete evidence of the effects from low doses of radiation, scientists have predicted effects based on studies of individuals and groups that received large doses of radiation. Our knowledge of effects from large exposures on humans was obtained from studies of the following:

- Early radiation workers who received large doses of radiation before scientists understood the biological effects and consequences. Exposure standards have since been established to protect workers and the public.
- 80,000 + survivors of the atomic bombs dropped in Hiroshima and Nagasaki. This large group has provided the most information on the effects of radiation.
- Cancer patients. Some patients receive large doses of radiation focused on a specific portion of the body to destroy cancerous cells. Although doctors try to avoid exposing healthy tissues, exposing healthy tissue adjacent to a tumor site is unavoidable.
- Radiation accident victims. Although small in number, we usually have detailed medical records from this group.

Information gained from years of radiation-related research has helped determine more specifically how ionizing radiation can damage the human body and what levels of exposure cause what kinds of damage. Based on these studies, we know more about the biological effects of ionizing radiation than we do about many other environmental hazards.

How Ionizing Radiation Affects the Body

Scientists have determined that the effects of ionizing radiation occur at the cellular level. The human body is made up of many organs, and each organ of the body is made up of specialized cells. Ionizing radiation can affect the normal operation of these cells.

The way radiation causes damage to any material is by ionizing the atoms in that material—changing the atomic structure of the material. When atoms are ionized, the chemical properties of those atoms are altered. This is how radiation can damage a cell; it ionizes the atoms and changes the resulting chemical behavior of the atoms and/or molecules in the cell. If a person receives a sufficiently high dose of radiation and many cells are damaged, there may be noticeable—observable—health effects.

The amount of the body exposed to radiation is a factor in determining the biological effect. While many cancer patients receive large doses of radiation to destroy tumors, this radiation is concentrated on a specific portion of the body. Exposing the whole body poses more risk because the radiation-induced damage affects a larger area.

Some parts of the body are more sensitive to radiation-induced damage than others. Radiation damage to the cells of the body depends on how sensitive the cells are to ionizing radiation. Generally speaking, the most sensitive cells are those that divide rapidly or those that are in the process of dividing. These cells are most vulnerable because it is difficult or impossible for them to repair any damage that may occur during cell division. Examples of rapidly dividing cells include:

- Blood-forming cells
- Cells lining the intestinal tract
- Cells in an embryo or fetus

Cells that divide more slowly and cells that are more specialized are not as easily damaged by ionizing radiation. Examples include:

- Nerve cells
- Brain cells
- Muscle cells

A special concern is the sensitivity of the developing embryo or fetus. The system of cells in the developing embryo or fetus is especially sensitive to ionizing radiation because they are unspecialized and rapidly dividing. In general, we become less sensitive to the effects of ionizing radiation with increasing age. The exception is later in life we become more sensitive because of a less effective cellular repair mechanism. People's health and genetics also play a part in determining what effect an exposure has.

Often, the biological effects of ionizing radiation depend on how much and how fast a radiation dose is received. There are two categories of radiation doses: acute radiation doses and chronic radiation doses.

Acute Doses

A large dose of radiation received in a short period of time is called an acute dose. The body can't repair or replace cells fast enough after a large acute dose of radiation, so physical effects may be seen. Some possible health effects from acute doses of radiation include reduced blood count, hair loss, nausea, and fatigue. The physical reaction to an acute dose of radiation is the result of extensive cell damage over a short period of time.

Radiation therapy patients (e.g., patients undergoing cancer treatment) receive high doses of radiation over a short period of time, generally applied to a small portion of the body. Ionizing radiation is used to treat cancer because cancer cells divide rapidly and are sensitive to ionizing radiation.

It takes a large acute dose of radiation before people experience any observable physical effects. Physical effects may take days to manifest themselves and may include nausea, vomiting, and diarrhea. Other than radiation therapy patients, acute doses have only been received by survivors exposed at Hiroshima and Nagasaki and by people at a few radiation incidents at nuclear facilities.

Most radioactive material shipments contain small amounts of radioactivity. Federal packaging regulations require that the level of radiation (measured on the external surface of shipping packages) be low enough that those who handle packages, or those who are potentially exposed to the package, will not experience any adverse

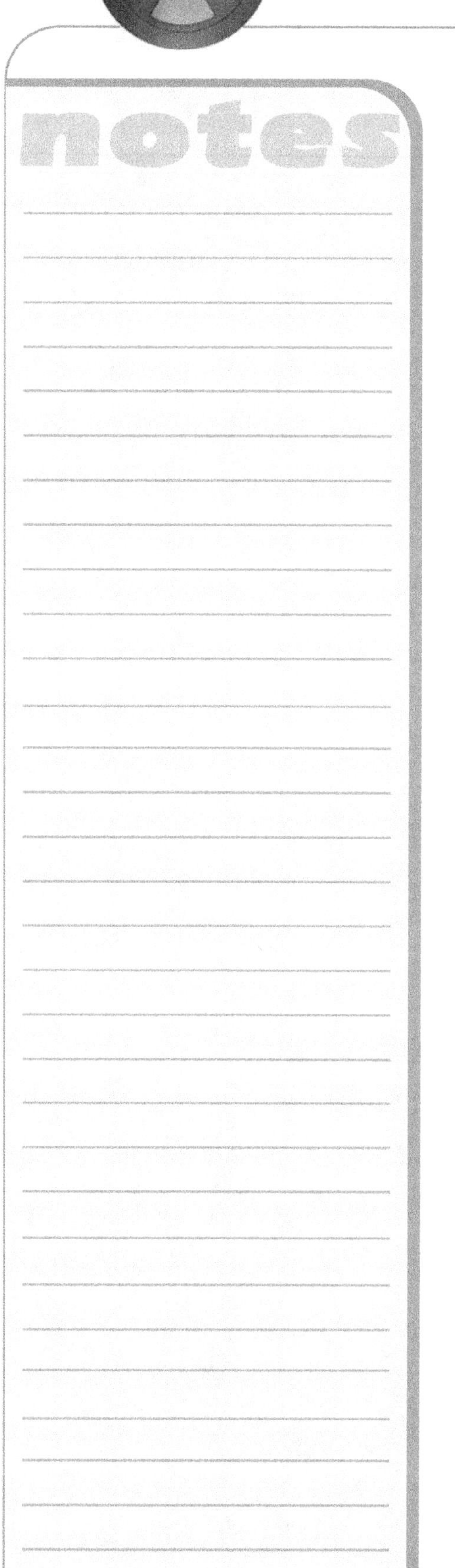

health effects. When highly radioactive material is shipped, special packages are used that have been designed to withstand severe accident conditions without breaching or releasing their radioactive contents.

The probability that you, as a responder, will receive an acute dose of radiation while responding to a transportation incident is extremely low.

Chronic Doses

A chronic dose of radiation is a small amount of radiation received over a long period of time. The body is better equipped to handle a chronic dose of radiation than it is an acute dose of radiation. The body can repair the damage from chronic doses because fewer cells will need repair at any given time. The body has enough time to replace dead or non-functioning cells with healthy ones.

Chronic doses do not result in the detectable health effects seen with acute doses. Because of cell repair, even a sophisticated blood analysis will not reveal any biological effects. Examples of chronic radiation doses include the everyday doses we receive from natural background radiation and the doses received by workers in nuclear and medical facilities.

EXPOSURE RISKS

Numerous scientific studies have shown that large non-lethal radiation doses delivered acutely (>10,000 millirem) can increase the risk of cancer. We don't know if this is true for low doses delivered over extended periods of time. The current philosophy of radiation protection is based on the assumption that any radiation dose, no matter how small, may result in human health effects such as cancer and genetic damage. Although this philosophy is simplistic and probably incorrect, it is conservative. The numerous epidemiological studies conducted to date show that health risks at doses below about 10,000 millirem are either zero or so low that they cannot be measured.

If you are interested in learning more, the National Health Physics Society website has a great deal of information on radiation and its biological effects. The web address is http://www.hps.org.

BIOLOGICAL PATHWAYS

Internal radioactive contamination results when radioactive material gets into the body. Your skin, mouth, and nose are the most obvious—and avoidable—routes to internal contamination. Radioactive material can enter the body through the same pathways as any other material.

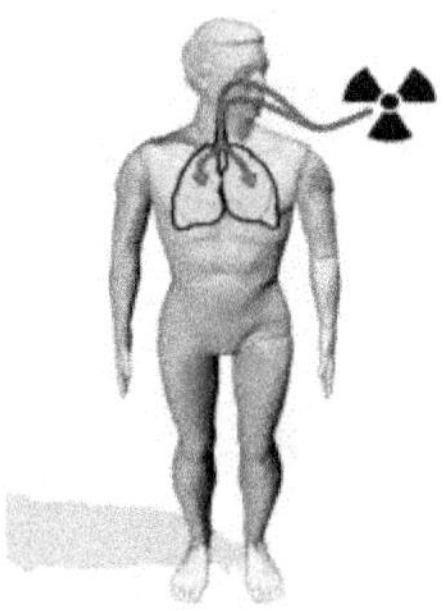

Biological pathways that can introduce internal contamination include:

Inhalation - smoke particles or other airborne particulate matter may enter the body through the lungs as you breathe.

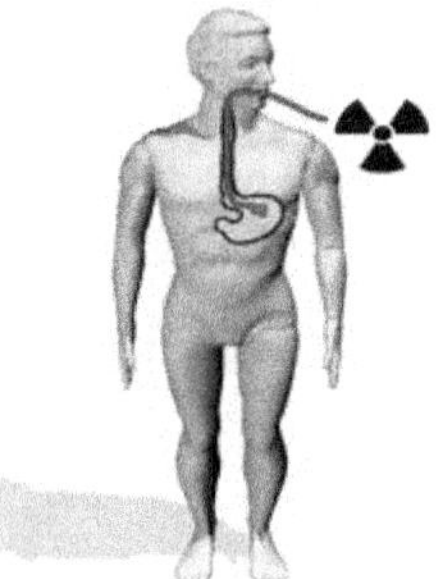

Ingestion - eating, drinking, smoking, or chewing contaminated items may cause internal radiological contamination.

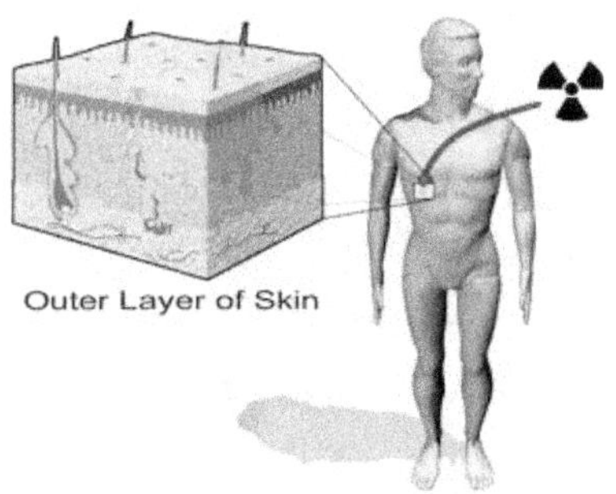

Absorption - radioactive material may be absorbed through the skin or mucous membranes the same way other things are absorbed.

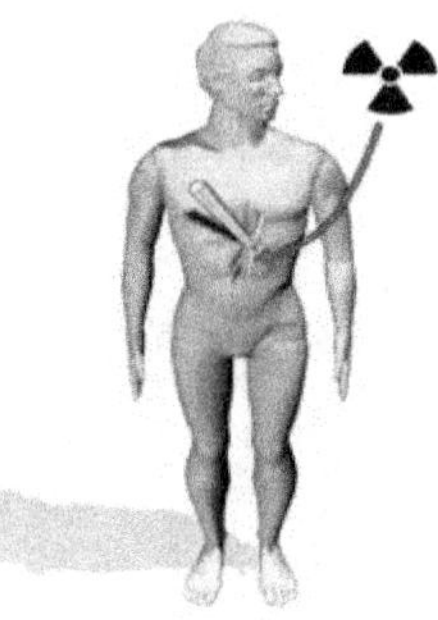

Injection - radioactive material can be introduced to the body through cuts, wounds, direct medical injections, or other punctures in the skin.

Check Your Understanding

1. The way radiation causes damage to any material is by _________ the atoms in that material—changing the atomic structure of the material.

2. If a sufficiently high dose of radiation is received, and a large number of cells are damaged, observable _________ may be seen.

3. A(n) _______ dose is a large dose received in a short period of time.

4. A(n) _______ dose is a small dose received in a continuous or long-term exposure.

5. One possible health effect from a large acute exposure to ionizing radiation is:
   a) Arthritis
   b) Hair loss
   c) Rapid onset of streptococcus
   d) Increased cranial capacity

6. List the pathways by which radioactive material can enter the body:
   ____
   ____
   ____
   ____

ANSWERS

1. ionizing
2. effects
3. acute
4. chronic
5. b
6. Inhalation
   Ingestion
   Absorption
   Injection

M E R R T T
Hazard Recognition

INTRODUCTION

Very strict regulations control the shipment of radioactive material. The regulations require that shipments of radioactive material be marked, labeled, or placarded. This information provides important details about the nature of the material being transported and may help you during an accident.

PURPOSE

The purpose of this module is to increase your understanding of package markings, warning labels, and placards used for packaging and shipping radioactive material.

As an emergency responder, you need to be aware of radioactive material present at an accident scene. Understanding radioactive material marking, labeling, and placarding requirements will help you properly assess accident scenes and respond appropriately.

MODULE OBJECTIVES

Upon completion of this module, you will be able to:

1. Identify markings on packages used to transport radioactive material.
2. Identify labels on packages used to indicate the presence of radioactive material.
3. Identify placards used on radioactive material shipments.

M E R R T T
Hazard Recognition

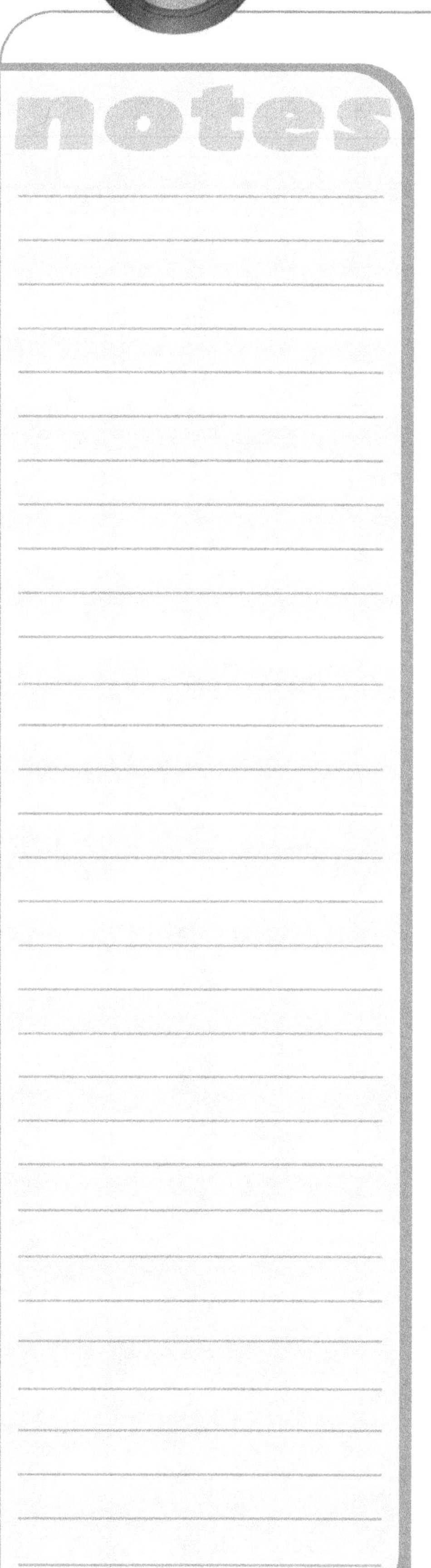

RADIOACTIVE MATERIAL: Shipping and Packaging Concerns

Safe Packaging

Prior to transport, regulations require that radioactive material be properly packaged, sealed, surveyed for external radiation, and then checked for external contamination. The package is then marked and labeled (as required) to communicate specific information about its contents.

Package Markings

Package markings are designed to inform transportation workers and emergency response personnel about the package's radioactive contents. Package markings will be clearly marked on the outside of the package. Some of the markings you may see on a radioactive material package include the following:

- Proper Shipping Name and UN identification number (e.g., Radioactive material, Type A package, UN 2915)
- "Radioactive LSA" or "Radioactive SCO"[1] (if applicable)
- "Type IP-1, IP-2, IP-3, or Type A" or "Type B"[2] (if applicable)
- Gross weight, if package weighs more than 110 lbs.
- "USA"
- Orientation arrows. This is a good indication that the package contains liquids (see figure below)
- "RQ" if the package contains a reportable quantity of material

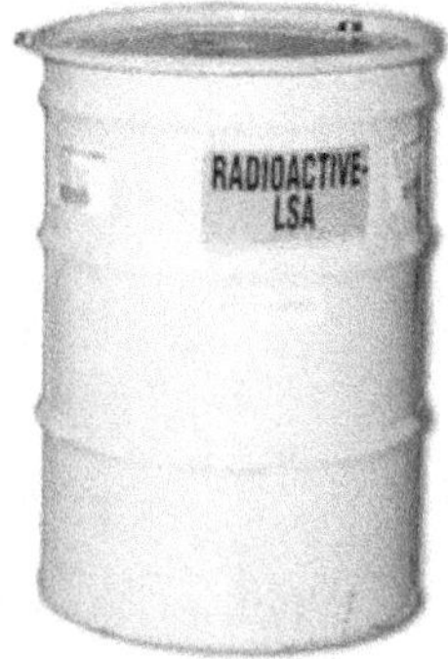

---

[1] Radioactive Low Specific Activity (LSA) and Surface Contaminated Objects (SCO) shipments, when transported exclusively on a conveyance may be excepted (exempt) from the other marking and labeling requirements discussed here. When excepted from these marking and labeling requirements, vehicle placarding is required. More information on LSA and SCO material is given in Module 8, Radiological Terminology and Units.

[2] Type IP-1, IP-2, IP-3, Type A, and Type B refer to specific types of radioactive material packaging. Package types are discussed in more detail in the Radioactive Material Shipping Packages module.

M E R R T T
Hazard Recognition

Radiation-warning Labels

Radioactive material packages may require special labels in addition to any marking required. The radioactive labels alert persons, particularly handlers, that the package contains radioactive material and that the package may require special handling and storage controls. Some radioactive material packages do not require labels. Bulk packages containing large volumes of low-level radioactive material may not require labels although vehicle placards may be required.

When required, labels must be applied to opposite sides of the package. Labels contain specific information about the quantity and type of radioactive material being shipped. The type of label used depends on the external radiation level or in some cases the package contents. The shipper must measure the radiation levels to determine which label is required.

The following labels may be used on packages used to transport radioactive material:

Radioactive White-I: minimal radiation levels detectable outside the package.

Radioactive Yellow-II: medium-level radiation levels detectable outside the package.

Radioactive Yellow-III: highest radiation levels detectable outside the package.

Fissile Label: applied to packages that contain fissile materials[3]. The Criticality Safety Index (CSI) for each package will be noted on the label. The CSI is displayed on the label to assist the shipper in controlling how many fissile packages can be grouped together on a conveyance. When applicable, the fissile label will appear adjacent to the radioactive material label.

EMPTY: applied to packages that have been emptied of their contents as far as practical but may still contain regulated amounts of internal contamination and minimal radiation levels detectable outside the package.

---

[3] Fissile materials are composed of atoms that can be split by neutrons in a self-sustaining chain-reaction (criticality) to release enormous amounts of energy. Special controls are placed on fissile materials during transportation to ensure nuclear criticality safety.

In a response situation, if you encounter a package that has a radiation-warning label on it, carefully note the specific label. Also note any other information or markings on the package. Write all the information down and be certain of its accuracy. As with all hazardous material, you need to have as much information as possible in a response situation.

Placarding Requirements

Not all shipments of radioactive material require that the transport vehicle be placarded. Rail or highway shipments containing excepted quantities and packages with the EMPTY, Radioactive White-I, and Radioactive Yellow-II labels do not require vehicle placarding. Placarding is required for the following:

- Packages with the Yellow-III label
- Exclusive Use[4] LSA/SCO shipments in excepted packages
- Highway Route Controlled Quantities of material

When required, placards must be in plain view and displayed on all four sides of the transport vehicle as show below.

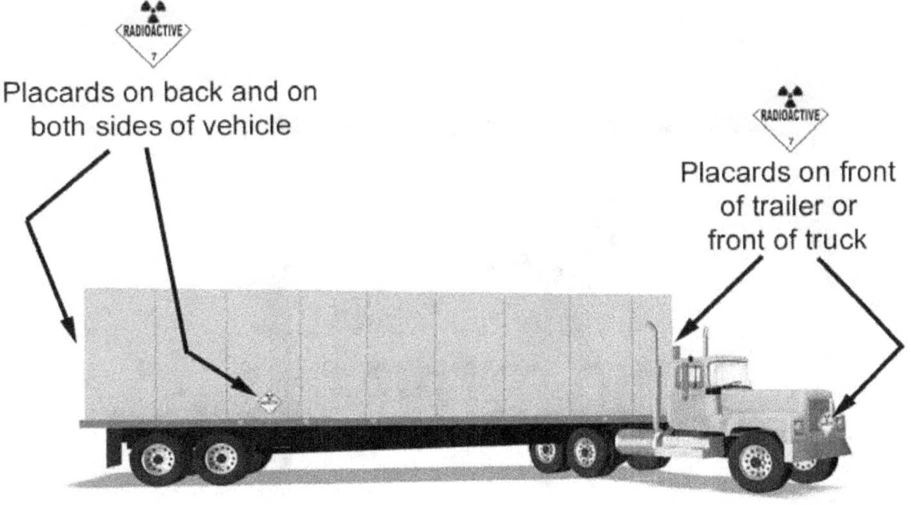

---

[4] "Exclusive use" means a single shipper transports the material and all initial, intermediate, and final loading and unloading are carried out in accordance with the direction of the shipper or receiver.

notes

The standard placard for radioactive material is square-on-point and is yellow on top and white on the bottom, with black lettering and a black radiation symbol in the yellow portion. Standard size is approximately 11 x 11 inches. In the bottom corner, the DOT hazard class number "7" denotes radioactive material.

There is one other type of radioactive placard that you may encounter on highway shipments. It looks like the standard placard, except that it has a white square background and a black border. This placard represents a "Highway Route Controlled Quantity" (HRCQ) shipment. HRCQ shipments contain higher quantities of radioactive material and require special controls during transport. Special controls include operating highway vehicles over "preferred routes."

A preferred route is the Interstate Highway system or a state-designated alternate route selected by a state agency. The driver of a HRCQ vehicle must be provided with a written route plan, must have received DOT mandated training within two years prior to the shipment, and must have a certificate of such training in his possession during the shipment.

United Nations Identification Number

In addition to the radioactive placard, the vehicle may also have a United Nations Identification Number (UN ID) located close to the placard. The UN ID number will appear on either an orange panel or on a plain white square-on-point configuration similar to a placard. The orange panel is orange with black lettering and has a four-digit identification number that identifies the radioactive material. This four-digit number is the UN identification number of the material being transported. The orange panel and white square-on-point configuration is used because UN identification numbers may not be displayed on a Class 7 placard. The UN identification number can be used to locate the name of the material and the response guide in the Emergency Response Guidebook (ERG).

Secondary Hazards

Responders should always be alert for the presence of secondary hazards at an incident site. These secondary hazards can come from other possible sources such as other hazardous material carried on the vehicle or external factors such as downed power lines, spilled fuel, etc. If you observe a radioactive placard, do not let this distract you from looking for additional placards on the vehicle. Be aware that some radioactive material may have other hazardous properties. For instance, they may be contained in a compressed gas or contain corrosive chemicals.

Remember that radioactive placards may not indicate the only hazard(s) on the vehicle. Don't get "tunnel vision" about radiation; it is important to look for spilled fuel, downed power lines, etc., since these may pose a more immediate hazard than the radioactive material.

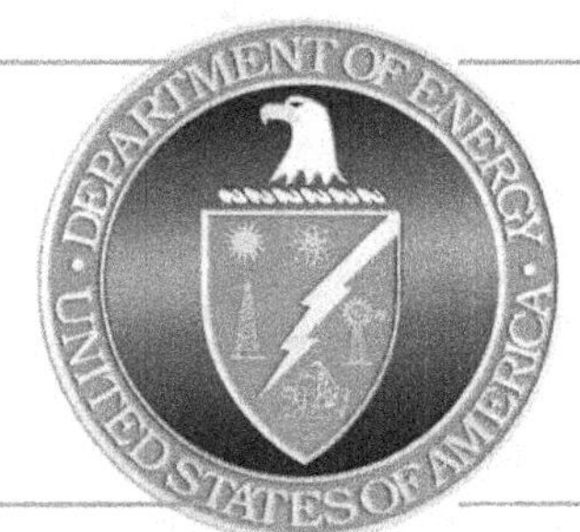

1. Package _________ and labels are designed to inform transportation workers and emergency response personnel about a package's radioactive contents.

2. Orientation arrows on the outside of a package are a good indication that the package contains __________.

3. All packages of radioactive material require radiation-warning labels. True/False.

4. Which of the following is true regarding the use of radiation-warning labels?
a) Radiation-warning labels are only used on medical shipments
b) When required, they will appear on opposite sides of the package
c) All shipments of radioactive material require radiation-warning labels
d) Radiation-warning labels are placed on vehicles transporting radioactive material

5. The _______ label is applied to packages that, after being emptied of their contents, may still contain a regulated amount of internal contamination.

6. Placarding is required on all shipments of radioactive material. True/False.

7. The standard placard for radioactive material is _______ on top and _________ on the bottom, with black lettering and a black radiation symbol. In the bottom corner, the DOT hazard class number __ denotes radioactive material.

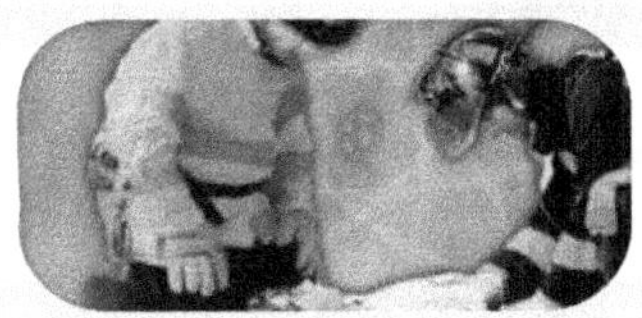
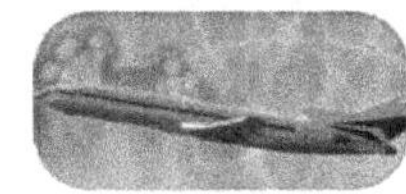
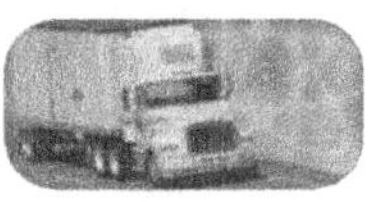

ANSWERS

1. markings
2. liquids
3. False
4. b
5. empty
6. False
7. yellow
   white
   7

INTRODUCTION

This module will provide you with information about the initial response actions you should take when arriving at the scene of a transportation incident involving radioactive material. You will learn how to use the U.S. Department of Transportation's Emergency Response Guidebook (ERG) and also how to isolate and control an accident scene.

You will also be able to identify medical priorities at a radioactive material transportation incident. This module should not be considered comprehensive training on how to use the ERG.

PURPOSE

The purpose of this module is to provide a basic understanding of the initial actions you should take when arriving at a scene of a radioactive material transportation incident.

Your ability to effectively identify the hazard using the ERG will enhance your efficiency in responding to the incident.

MODULE OBJECTIVES

Upon completion of this module, you will be able to:

1. Identify the actions required by "Safety, Isolation, and Notification."
2. Identify the information contained on shipping papers used for transporting radioactive material.
3. Locate, in the U.S. Department of Transportation Emergency Response Guidebook (ERG), the response guide for radioactive material by using one or all of the following: UN identification number, material name, or shipment placards.

INITIAL RESPONSE ACTIONS

State, tribal, and local government officials are responsible for providing emergency response to any incident within their jurisdiction, including those involving radioactive material. To successfully deal with transportation incidents involving radioactive material, state, tribal, and local government officials should develop a response plan for these incidents. This plan should be developed before an incident occurs.

If an incident involving radioactive material occurs in your jurisdiction, follow your local and or state emergency response procedures. If your local agency does not have procedures in place, the U.S. Department of Energy has a TEPP Model Initial Response Procedure available.[1]

Safety, Isolation, and Notification

In order for you to effectively carry out your duties as a responder, your protection and safety should be foremost. This should always be your first operational thought at any hazardous material incident scene. A useful acronym to help remember your initial response actions is "SIN." SIN stands for:

Safety first and always
Isolate and deny entry
Notifications

[1] Information can be found on the Department of Energy's web site:
http://web.em.doe.gov/otem/program.html

M E R R T T
Initial Response Actions

1. Safety First and Always

Approaching an incident involving radioactive material is not significantly different from approaching an incident involving other hazardous material. To ensure your safety, you should always attempt to approach the incident scene from upwind and upslope, trying to identify the hazard from as far away as possible, using binoculars if available. Use the ERG to determine your initial isolation distances.

Once you've ensured your own safety at the scene, your priorities should be for rescue, life saving, first aid, and fire control. According to the ERG, all these priorities are "higher than the priority for measuring radiation levels." All of the guides covering radioactive material in the ERG state that "radiation presents minimal risk to transport workers, emergency response personnel, and the public during transportation accidents."

If you need to enter the area to perform rescue operations, you can minimize your radiation exposure by following a few "common sense" guidelines:

■ Minimize your **time** in the incident area. The less time you spend in a radiation field, the less radiation dose you will receive.

- Maintain a safe **distance** from radioactive material packages. Do not touch damaged packages or spilled material.
- Use other available material for **shielding** whenever possible. A vehicle between you and the radiation source can reduce your radiation exposure (e.g., ambulance, patrol car, fire pumper, etc.).

2. **Isolate and Deny Entry to the Area**

When responding to a transportation incident involving radioactive material, isolate the scene to reduce the potential for spreading radioactive contamination and to minimize possible radiation exposure. Guides 161 through 166 in the ERG can be used to determine initial isolation distances. These guides recommend an initial isolation of 75 feet in all directions. Responders at any hazardous material scene should keep unauthorized personnel away from the area and always try to position themselves uphill, upwind, and upstream of the incident.

If life saving, first aid, or control of fire is not necessary at an incident scene, there is no need for a responder to enter the area. Avoid the urge to go in and "look around." Once the area is isolated, deny entry and wait for members of the hazardous material response team, state radiological control, or other trained personnel to arrive.

M E R R T T
Initial Response Actions

Once the area is isolated, try to identify the material involved in the incident; you can refer to the ERG to help identify the material and determine the appropriate immediate steps to take. An overview of the ERG is included in this module.

3. Begin the Notification Process

When a hazardous material incident of any kind occurs, notify the proper agencies and personnel as soon as possible. Most states have a radiological health agency. The state radiological health agency may be able to provide additional assistance/resources for a radioactive material related incident. The agency can either provide specialized assistance, or identify other available resources. If you are the first person to arrive on the scene of a radioactive material incident, follow your state or local notification procedure. Your local notification procedure may be similar to this:

Call Dispatch/911

- Ask dispatch to make any other necessary contacts, including:
  - Other local personnel that may be needed
  - State radiological agency
  - Neighboring jurisdictions that may be affected

M E R R T T
Initial Response Actions

- Include the following information in your notification to dispatch:
  - Your name, agency, and call-back number
  - Radioactive material(s) involved, and type(s) of package(s)
  - Severity of the incident (injuries, breached packages)
  - Incident location
  - Actions already taken
  - On-scene contact (Incident Commander), and how to reach this person
  - How the incident occurred
  - Carrier, shipper, and receiver information (from shipping papers or packages)

- Contact the emergency response telephone number listed on the shipping papers.

- Other notifications: this varies with each organization.

Shipping Papers

The driver of the transport vehicle, if available, can be a valuable source of information about the nature of the material being transported. The driver may also be of assistance when retrieving the shipping papers. The shipping papers contain valuable information on the material being transported. They include the name, address, and telephone number for both the shipper and receiver and contain specific information on the nature of the radioactive contents.

The shipping papers must provide an emergency response telephone number, including the area code or international access code, for use in the event of an emergency involving the material. The person answering the phone must be knowledgeable of the material and mitigation actions to be taken, or must have immediate access to a person who has the required knowledge.

Shipping papers are required for all modes of transport. Drivers of motor vehicles transporting hazardous material are required to have shipping papers readily available to response personnel. A vehicle's

shipping papers are usually found in a holder mounted on the inside of the driver's side door, or within arm's reach of the driver. When the driver is not in the vehicle, the shipping papers must be placed on the driver's seat. Though shipping papers are important, they should not be retrieved at the expense of safety. No responder should compromise their own safety to retrieve shipping papers.

If you can retrieve shipping papers without significant risk, you should do so at the earliest opportunity. Information found on shipping papers that is specific to radioactive material includes:

- Identity of each material/radionuclide (e.g., Mo-99, Tl-201, I-123)
- Physical and chemical form of each material (e.g., salt/solid)
- The amount of radioactivity contained in each package
- Category of label applied to each package (e.g., Radioactive Yellow-II)
- Assigned transport index for each package (applies to Yellow-II and Yellow-III labels only)
- Fissile controls information[2] (if applicable)

Depending on the mode of transport, shipping papers may be located in any of the following places:

- In the cab of the motor vehicle
- In the possession of a train crew member
- In a holder on the bridge of a vessel
- In the possession of an aircraft's pilot

---

[2] Applies to material labeled as FISSILE. These materials have the capability of undergoing fission (splitting of atom's nucleus) and thus require controls to assure nuclear criticality safety during transport.

M E R R T T
Initial Response Actions

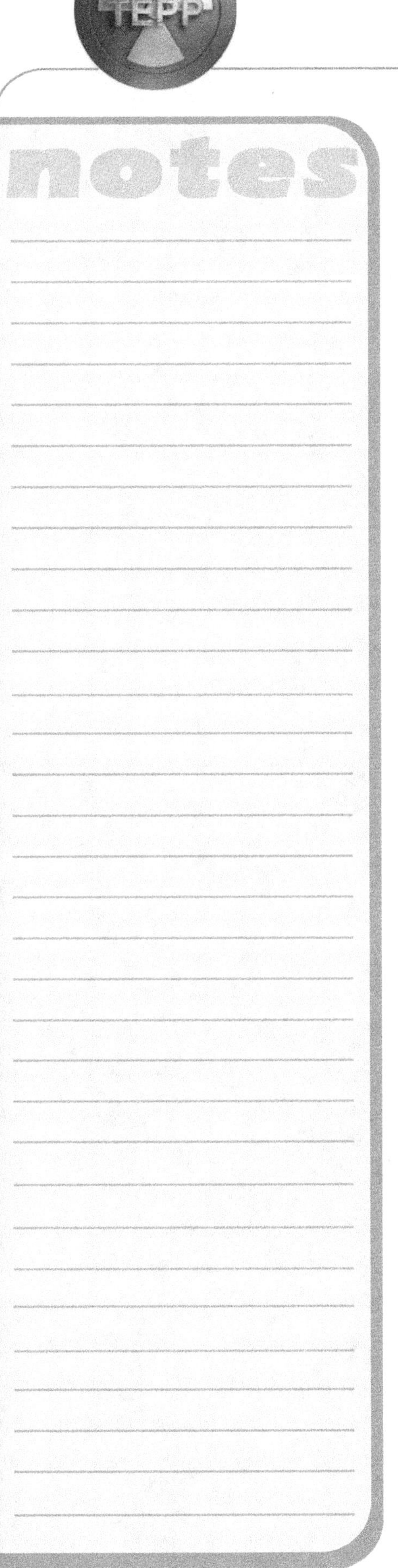

Handling Potentially Contaminated Shipping Papers

If you suspect that the shipping papers are contaminated, the following steps can be used to prevent the spread of contamination when removing shipping papers from the hot zone.

In the hot zone, and with the protection of appropriate Personal Protective Equipment (PPE):

- Separate each page
- Carefully wipe off any liquid or other material from the shipping papers' surfaces
- Place each page into a separate plastic bag. (Clear food storage bags work well; they lay flat and are large enough to hold a flat 8.5" x 11" sheet)
- Pass bags through the decontamination line and decontaminate (decon) the outside of each bag by wiping it off
- In the clean zone, place another plastic bag over the outside of the original bag
- Handle the documents carefully until they can be monitored for contamination. If possible, make photocopies of the documents (through the bags) and place the originals in a safe location

EMERGENCY RESPONSE GUIDEBOOK (ERG) OVERVIEW

The ERG provides guidelines for responders to use for commonly transported hazardous material, including radioactive material. The guides for radioactive material are numbered 161-166.

Remember that the ERG is only a guidebook and should not take precedence over local standard operating procedures.

The ERG is intended to help you make informed decisions about the type of hazards involved and the initial precautions to take. To use the ERG effectively, you should become familiar with the ERG **prior** to an emergency.

The guidebook lists the four-digit United Nations Identification Number (UN ID) used on shipping papers, package markings and some placards as well as the Proper Shipping Names of hazardous material. Each hazard has a guide and precautions designed to protect responders from harm. The guidebook also lists common placards used in the transportation of hazardous material.

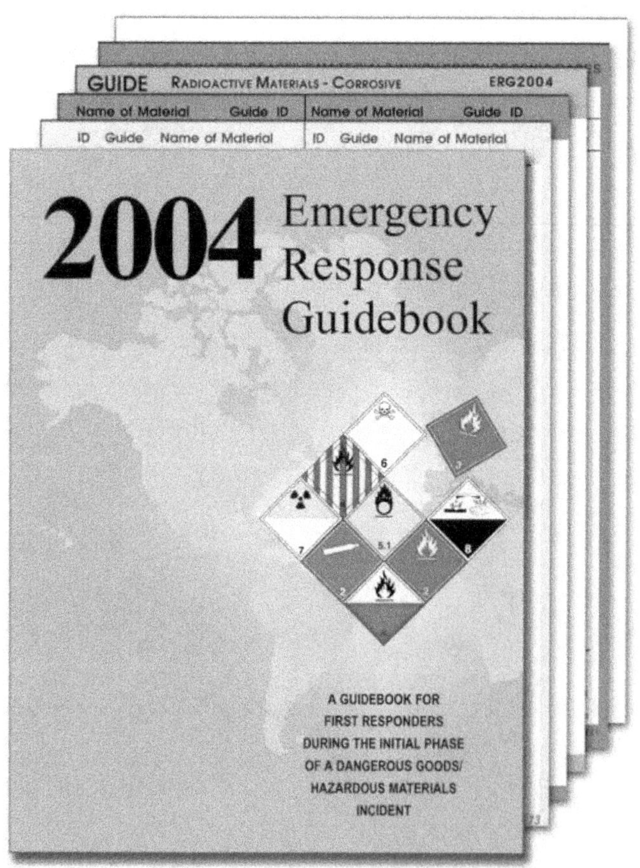

Overview of color-coded sections:

The initial section is **white** and contains general guidelines for any hazardous material situation. It addresses safety precautions and who to call for assistance. The initial white section also contains the "table of placards and initial response guides." The table of placards displays the placards used on transport vehicles carrying dangerous goods.

You can refer to the table of placards and initial response guides if you respond to an incident involving placarded material but are unsure of what material is represented by the placard. Match the vehicle placard(s) with one of the placards displayed on the table of placards. A numbered guide is located next to each placard in the table and is shown as a circled number next to each placard. Use this guide number until the hazardous material involved can be specifically identified.

For radioactive material, package labels and placards used on shipments are shown in the table of placards. As the detail below illustrates, if you see a radioactive label or placard pictured and have no other information, you can determine which guide number to use (Guide 163) by looking at the circled number next to the radioactive label and placard on the table (*see example below*).

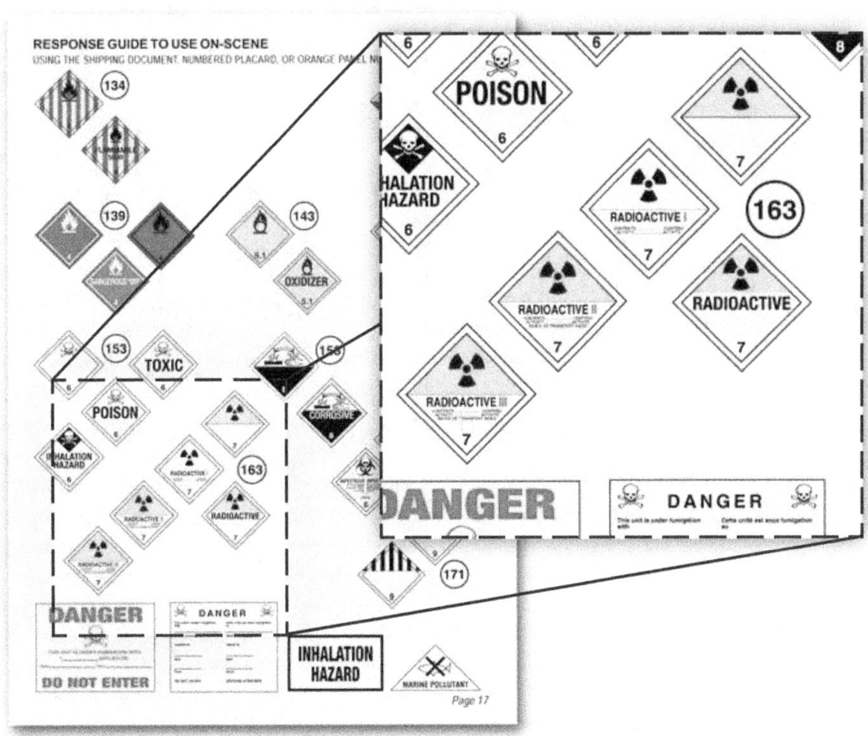

The **yellow** section shows, in numerical order, the four-digit UN ID number assigned to each hazardous material. By looking up the UN ID number, you can find the appropriate guide number and name of the hazardous material. For example, if you were looking up UN ID number 2977, you would find that the name of the material is "Radioactive material, Uranium hexafluoride, fissile" and that the guide number is 166 (*See below*).

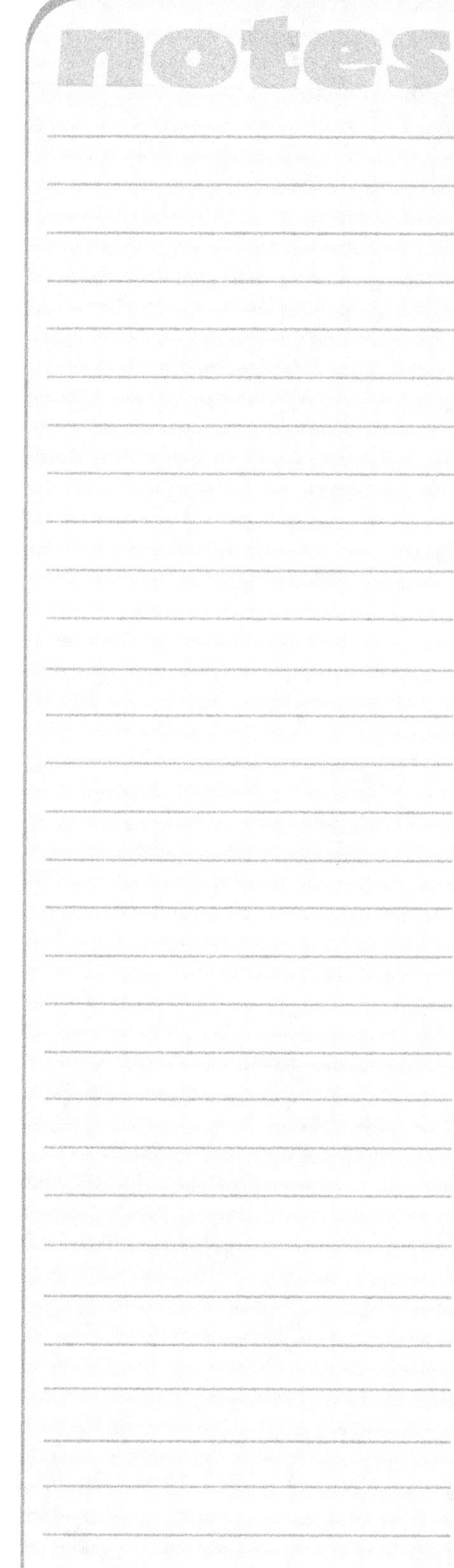

ID No.	Guide No.	Name of Material
2966	153	Thioglycol
2967	154	Sulfamic acid
2967	154	Sulphamic acid
2968	135	Maneb, stabilized
2968	135	Maneb preparation, stabilized
2969	171	Castor beans, meal, pomace or flake
2974	164	Radioactive material, special form, n.o.s.
2975	162	Thorium metal, pyrophoric
2976	162	Thorium nitrate, solid
2977	166	Radioactive material, Uranium hexafluoride, fissile
2977	166	Uranium hexafluoride, fissile containing more than 1% Uranium-235
2978	166	Radioactive material, Uranium hexafluoride
2978	166	Radioactive material, Uranium hexafluoride, non-fissile or fissile-excepted
2978	166	Uranium hexafluoride
2978	166	Uranium hexafluoride, fissile-excepted
2978	166	Uranium hexafluoride, low specific activity
2978	166	Uranium hexafluoride, non-fissile
2979	162	Uranium metal, pyrophoric
2980	162	Uranium nitrate, hexahydrate, solution
2980	162	Uranyl nitrate, hexahydrate, solution
2981	162	Uranyl nitrate, solid
2982	163	Radioactive material, n.o.s.
2983	129P	Ethylene oxide and Propylene oxide mixture, with not more than 30% Ethylene oxide
2983	129P	Propylene oxide and Ethylene oxide mixture, with not more than 30% Ethylene oxide
2984	140	Hydrogen peroxide, aqueous solution, with not less than 8% but less than 20% Hydrogen peroxide
2985	155	Chlorosilanes, flammable, corrosive, n.o.s.
2985	155	Chlorosilanes, n.o.s.
2986	155	Chlorosilanes, corrosive, flammable, n.o.s.
2986	155	Chlorosilanes, n.o.s.
2987	156	Chlorosilanes, corrosive, n.o.s.
2987	156	Chlorosilanes, n.o.s.
2988	139	Chlorosilanes, n.o.s.
2988	139	Chlorosilanes, water-reactive, flammable, corrosive, n.o.s.
2989	133	Lead phosphite, dibasic
2990	171	Life-saving appliances, self-inflating
2991	131	Carbamate pesticide, liquid, poisonous, flammable
2991	131	Carbamate pesticide, liquid, toxic, flammable
2992	151	Carbamate pesticide, liquid, poisonous
2992	151	Carbamate pesticide, liquid, toxic
2993	131	Arsenical pesticide, liquid, poisonous, flammable
2993	131	Arsenical pesticide, liquid, toxic, flammable

Page 73

notes

The **blue** section alphabetically lists each hazardous material by Proper Shipping Name. By looking up the name of the material in this section, you can locate the appropriate guide number and UN ID number for it. For example, if you look up "Radioactive material, Uranium hexafluoride, fissile" you find, again, that the Guide number is 166 and that the UN ID number is 2977 (*See below*).

Name of Material	Guide No.	ID No.	Name of Material	Guide No.	ID No.
Radioactive material, low specific activity (LSA-II), fissile	165	3324	Radioactive material, Type B(M) package, fissile	165	3329
Radioactive material, low specific activity (LSA-III)	162	3322	Radioactive material, Type B(U) package	163	2916
Radioactive material, low specific activity (LSA-III), fissile	165	3325	Radioactive material, Type B(U) package, fissile	165	3328
Radioactive material, n.o.s.	163	2982	Radioactive material, Type C package	163	3323
Radioactive material, special form, n.o.s.	164	2974	Radioactive material, Type C package, fissile	165	3330
Radioactive material, surface contaminated objects (SCO)	162	2913	Radioactive material, Uranium hexafluoride, fissile	166	2977
Radioactive material, surface contaminated objects (SCO-I)	162	2913	Radioactive material, Uranium hexafluoride	166	2978
Radioactive material, surface contaminated objects (SCO-I), fissile	165	3326	Radioactive material, Uranium hexafluoride, non-fissile or fissile-excepted	166	2978
Radioactive material, surface contaminated objects (SCO-II)	162	2913	Rags, oily	133	1856
Radioactive material, surface contaminated objects (SCO-II), fissile	165	3326	Rare gases and Nitrogen mixture	121	1981
			Rare gases and Nitrogen mixture, compressed	121	1981
Radioactive material, transported under special arrangement	163	2919	Rare gases and Oxygen mixture	121	1980
Radioactive material, transported under special arrangement, fissile	165	3331	Rare gases and Oxygen mixture, compressed	121	1980
			Rare gases mixture	121	1979
Radioactive material, Type A package	163	2915	Rare gases mixture, compressed	121	1979
Radioactive material, Type A package, fissile	165	3327	Receptacles, small, containing gas	115	2037
Radioactive material, Type A package, special form	164	3332	Red phosphorus	133	1338
			Red phosphorus, amorphous	133	1338
Radioactive material, Type A package, special form, fissile	165	3333	Refrigerant gas, n.o.s.	126	1078
			Refrigerant gas, n.o.s. (flammable)	115	1954
Radioactive material, Type B(M) package	163	2917	Refrigerant gas R-12	126	1028
			Refrigerant gas R-12 and Refrigerant gas R-152a azeotropic mixture with 74% Refrigerant gas R-12	126	2602

Page 152

M E R R T T
Initial Response Actions

The **orange** section contains the guides for dealing with each material. These guides list the precautions to take for each hazardous material. The guides identify potential hazards (health, and fire or explosion) and emergency actions (initial, fire, spill or leak, and first aid) associated with each material. Each guide is two pages. Guide 166 is shown below and on the following page.

GUIDE 166	RADIOACTIVE MATERIALS - CORROSIVE (URANIUM HEXAFLUORIDE/WATER-SENSITIVE)	ERG2004

POTENTIAL HAZARDS

HEALTH
- Radiation presents minimal risk to transport workers, emergency response personnel and the public during transportation accidents. Packaging durability increases as potential radiation and criticality hazards of the content increase.
- Chemical hazard greatly exceeds radiation hazard.
- Substance reacts with water and water vapor in air to form toxic and corrosive hydrogen fluoride gas and an extremely irritating and corrosive, white-colored, water-soluble residue.
- If inhaled, may be fatal.
- Direct contact causes burns to skin, eyes, and respiratory tract.
- Low-level radioactive material; very low radiation hazard to people.
- Runoff from control of cargo fire may cause low-level pollution.

FIRE OR EXPLOSION
- Substance does not burn.   • The material may react violently with fuels.
- Containers in protective overpacks (horizontal cylindrical shape with short legs for tie-downs), are identified with "AF", "B(U)F" or "H(U)" on shipping papers or by markings on the overpacks. They are designed and evaluated to withstand severe conditions including total engulfment in flames at temperatures of 800°C (1475°F).
- Bare filled cylinders, identified with UN2978 as part of the marking (may also be marked H(U) or H(M)), may rupture in heat of engulfing fire; bare empty (except for residue) cylinders will not rupture in fires.
- Radioactivity does not change flammability or other properties of materials.

PUBLIC SAFETY
- **CALL Emergency Response Telephone Number on Shipping Paper first. If Shipping Paper not available or no answer, refer to appropriate telephone number listed on the inside back cover.**
- **Priorities for rescue, life-saving, first aid, fire control and other hazards are higher than the priority for measuring radiation levels.**
- Radiation Authority must be notified of accident conditions. Radiation Authority is usually responsible for decisions about radiological consequences and closure of emergencies.
- As an immediate precautionary measure, isolate spill or leak area for at least 25 meters (75 feet) in all directions.   • Stay upwind.   • Keep unauthorized personnel away.
- Detain or isolate uninjured persons or equipment suspected to be contaminated; delay decontamination and cleanup until instructions are received from Radiation Authority.

PROTECTIVE CLOTHING
- Wear positive pressure self-contained breathing apparatus (SCBA).
- Wear chemical protective clothing that is specifically recommended by the manufacturer. It may provide little or no thermal protection.
- Structural firefighters' protective clothing provides limited protection in fire situations ONLY; it is not effective in spill situations where direct contact with the substance is possible.

EVACUATION
Large Spill
- See the Table of Initial Isolation and Protective Action Distances.
Fire
- When a large quantity of this material is involved in a major fire, consider an initial evacuation distance of 300 meters (1000 feet) in all directions.

Page 280

M E R R T T
Initial Response Actions

notes

Page 2 of Guide 166 lists the emergency actions for fire, spill or leak, and first aid.

ERG2004	RADIOACTIVE MATERIALS - CORROSIVE (URANIUM HEXAFLUORIDE/WATER-SENSITIVE)	GUIDE 166

EMERGENCY RESPONSE

FIRE
- DO NOT USE WATER OR FOAM ON MATERIAL ITSELF.
- Move containers from fire area if you can do it without risk.

Small Fires
- Dry chemical or CO_2.

Large Fires
- Water spray, fog or regular foam.
- Cool containers with flooding quantities of water until well after fire is out.
- If this is impossible, withdraw from area and let fire burn.
- ALWAYS stay away from tanks engulfed in fire.

SPILL OR LEAK
- Do not touch damaged packages or spilled material.
- Without fire or smoke, leak will be evident by visible and irritating vapors and residue forming at the point of release.
- Use fine water spray to reduce vapors; do not put water directly on point of material release from container.
- Residue buildup may self-seal small leaks.
- Dike far ahead of spill to collect runoff water.

FIRST AID
- Medical problems take priority over radiological concerns.
- Use first aid treatment according to the nature of the injury.
- Do not delay care and transport of a seriously injured person.
- Give artificial respiration if victim is not breathing.
- Administer oxygen if breathing is difficult.
- In case of contact with substance, immediately flush skin or eyes with running water for at least 20 minutes.
- Effects of exposure (inhalation, ingestion or skin contact) to substance may be delayed.
- Injured persons contaminated by contact with released material are not a serious hazard to health care personnel, equipment or facilities.
- Ensure that medical personnel are aware of the material(s) involved, take precautions to protect themselves and prevent spread of contamination.

Page 281

The **green** section contains the table of initial isolation and protective action distances. These distances are useful for protecting people from vapors resulting from spills considered poisonous or toxic if inhaled. If you find an index entry is highlighted in the yellow or blue sections, look for the UN ID number and name of the material in the table of initial isolation and protective action distances. If necessary, begin protective actions immediately.

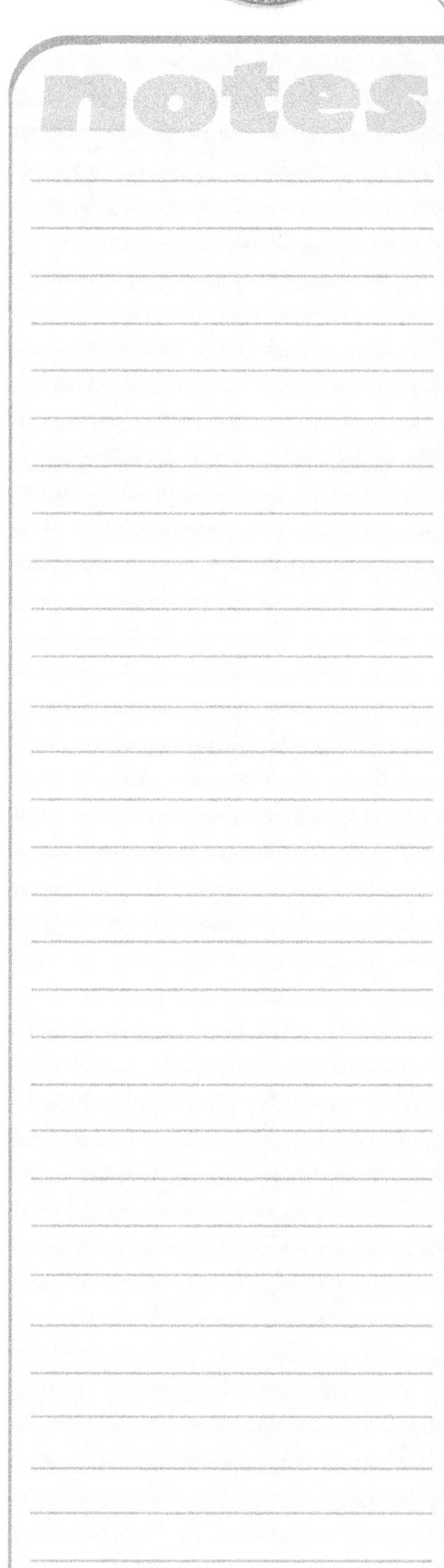

TABLE OF INITIAL ISOLATION AND PROTECTIVE ACTION DISTANCES

ID No.	NAME OF MATERIAL	SMALL SPILLS (From a small package or small leak from a large package) First ISOLATE in all Directions Meters (Feet)	SMALL SPILLS Then PROTECT persons Downwind during- DAY Kilometers (Miles)	SMALL SPILLS Then PROTECT persons Downwind during- NIGHT Kilometers (Miles)	LARGE SPILLS (From a large package or from many small packages) First ISOLATE in all Directions Meters (Feet)	LARGE SPILLS Then PROTECT persons Downwind during- DAY Kilometers (Miles)	LARGE SPILLS Then PROTECT persons Downwind during- NIGHT Kilometers (Miles)
2929	Toxic liquid, flammable, organic, n.o.s. (Inhalation Hazard Zone B)	60 m (200 ft)	0.4 km (0.2 mi)	1.0 km (0.6 mi)	270 m (900 ft)	2.5 km (1.6 mi)	5.6 km (3.5 mi)
2977	Radioactive material, Uranium hexafluoride, fissile **(when spilled in water)**	30 m (100 ft)	0.1 km (0.1 mi)	0.6 km (0.4 mi)	90 m (300 ft)	0.7 km (0.5 mi)	3.3 km (2.1 mi)
2977	Uranium hexafluoride, fissile containing more than 1% Uranium-235 **(when spilled in water)**						
2978	Radioactive material, Uranium hexafluoride **(when spilled in water)**	30 m (100 ft)	0.1 km (0.1 mi)	0.6 km (0.4 mi)	90 m (300 ft)	0.7 km (0.5 mi)	3.3 km (2.1 mi)
2978	Radioactive material, Uranium hexafluoride, non-fissile or fissile-excepted **(when spilled in water)**						
2978	Uranium hexafluoride **(when spilled in water)**						
2978	Uranium hexafluoride, fissile-excepted **(when spilled in water)**						
2978	Uranium hexafluoride, low specific activity **(when spilled in water)**						
2978	Uranium hexafluoride, non-fissile **(when spilled in water)**						
2985	Chlorosilanes, flammable, corrosive, n.o.s. **(when spilled in water)**	30 m (100 ft)	0.1 km (0.1 mi)	0.5 km (0.3 mi)	150 m (500 ft)	1.3 km (0.8 mi)	3.9 km (2.4 mi)
2985	Chlorosilanes, n.o.s. **(when spilled in water)**						

notes

Additionally, If the words "(when spilled in water)" also appear in conjunction with the material listed in the green section, this is an indication that the material is water reactive and is listed at the end of the green section in the "Table of Water-Reactive Materials Which Produce Toxic Gasses" section. Uranium Hexafluoride, for example, is listed in the "Table of Water-Reactive Materials Which Produce Toxic Gasses" section as a material which produces hydrogen fluoride gas when spilled in water.

TABLE OF WATER-REACTIVE MATERIALS WHICH PRODUCE TOXIC GASES

Materials Which Produce Large Amounts of Toxic-by-Inhalation (TIH) Gas(es) When Spilled in Water

ID No.	Guide No.	Name of Material	TIH Gas(es) Produced
2004	135	Magnesium diamide	NH_3
2011	139	Magnesium phosphide	PH_3
2012	139	Potassium phosphide	PH_3
2013	139	Strontium phosphide	PH_3
2437	156	Methylphenyldichlorosilane	HCl
2495	144	Iodine pentafluoride	HF
2691	137	Phosphorus pentabromide	HBr
2692	157	Boron tribromide	HBr
2806	138	Lithium nitride	NH_3
2977	166	Radioactive material, Uranium hexafluoride, fissile	HF
2977	166	Uranium hexafluoride, fissile containing more than 1% Uranium-235	HF
2978	166	Radioactive material, Uranium hexafluoride	HF
2978	166	Radioactive material, Uranium hexafluoride, non-fissile or fissile-excepted	HF
2978	166	Uranium hexafluoride	HF
2978	166	Uranium hexafluoride, fissile-excepted	HF
2978	166	Uranium hexafluoride, low specific activity	HF
2978	166	Uranium hexafluoride, non-fissile	HF
2985	155	Chlorosilanes, flammable, corrosive, n.o.s.	HCl
2985	155	Chlorosilanes, n.o.s.	HCl
2986	155	Chlorosilanes, corrosive, flammable, n.o.s.	HCl
2986	155	Chlorosilanes, n.o.s.	HCl
2987	156	Chlorosilanes, corrosive, n.o.s.	HCl
2987	156	Chlorosilanes, n.o.s.	HCl

Chemical Symbols for TIH Gases:

Br_2	Bromine	HF	Hydrogen fluoride	PH_3	Phosphine
Cl_2	Chlorine	HI	Hydrogen iodide	SO_2	Sulfur dioxide
HBr	Hydrogen bromide	H_2S	Hydrogen sulfide	SO_2	Sulphur dioxide
HCl	Hydrogen chloride	H_2S	Hydrogen sulphide	SO_3	Sulfur trioxide
HCN	Hydrogen cyanide	NH_3	Ammonia	SO_3	Sulphur trioxide

Use this list only when material is spilled in water.   *Page 347*

The final white section contains information on protective clothing as well as fire and spill control methods. Also included is information about criminal/terrorist use of chemical/biological/radiological agents including the differences between a chemical and a biological agent, indicators of a possible chemical incident, indicators of a possible biological incident, indicators of a possible radiological incident, personal safety considerations, and decontamination measures. The final white section also contains a glossary of terms.

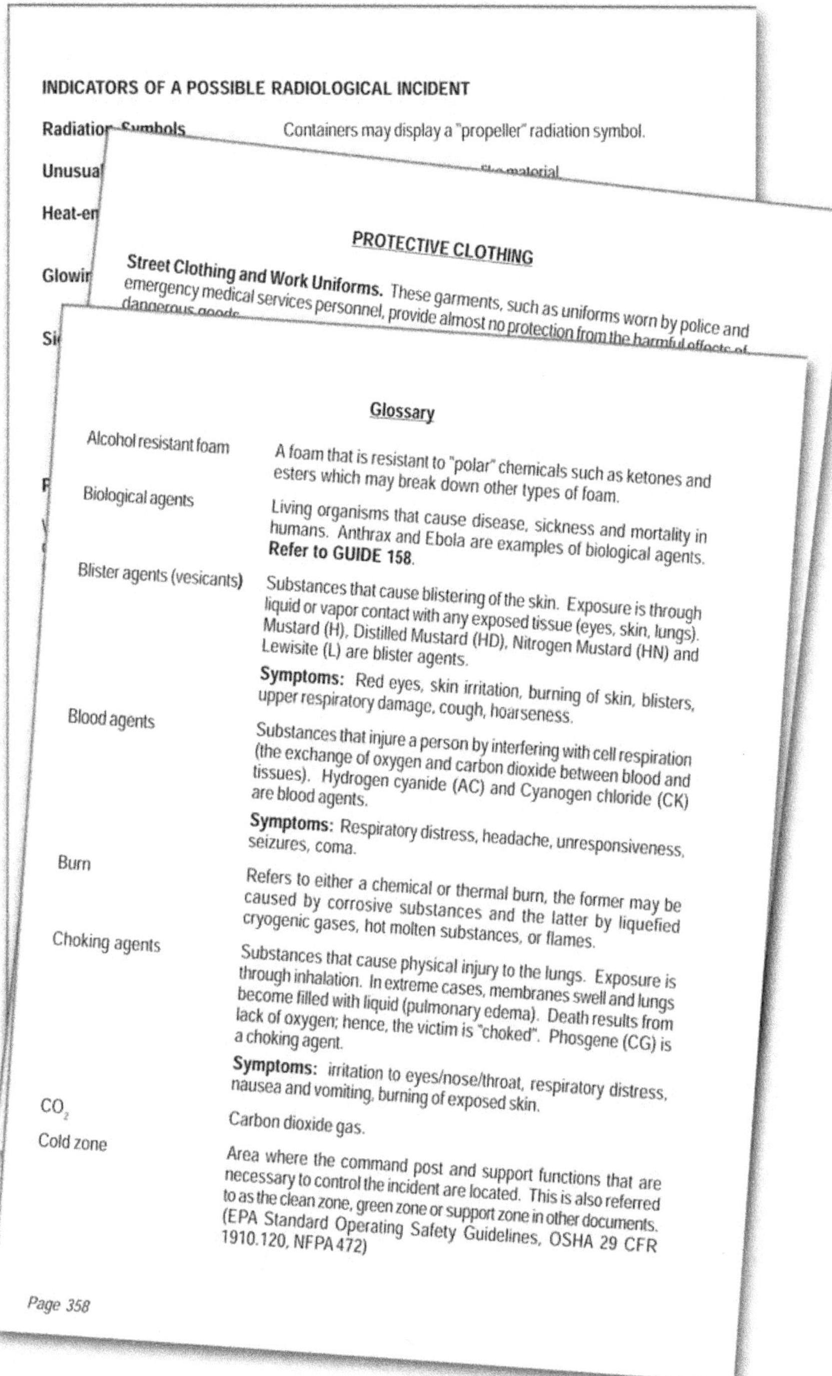

INDICATORS OF A POSSIBLE RADIOLOGICAL INCIDENT

Radiation Symbols — Containers may display a "propeller" radiation symbol.

Unusual ...

Heat-em ...

Glowin ...

Si ...

PROTECTIVE CLOTHING

Street Clothing and Work Uniforms. These garments, such as uniforms worn by police and emergency medical services personnel, provide almost no protection from the harmful effects of dangerous goods.

Glossary

Alcohol resistant foam	A foam that is resistant to "polar" chemicals such as ketones and esters which may break down other types of foam.
Biological agents	Living organisms that cause disease, sickness and mortality in humans. Anthrax and Ebola are examples of biological agents. **Refer to GUIDE 158**.
Blister agents (vesicants)	Substances that cause blistering of the skin. Exposure is through liquid or vapor contact with any exposed tissue (eyes, skin, lungs). Mustard (H), Distilled Mustard (HD), Nitrogen Mustard (HN) and Lewisite (L) are blister agents. **Symptoms:** Red eyes, skin irritation, burning of skin, blisters, upper respiratory damage, cough, hoarseness.
Blood agents	Substances that injure a person by interfering with cell respiration (the exchange of oxygen and carbon dioxide between blood and tissues). Hydrogen cyanide (AC) and Cyanogen chloride (CK) are blood agents. **Symptoms:** Respiratory distress, headache, unresponsiveness, seizures, coma.
Burn	Refers to either a chemical or thermal burn, the former may be caused by corrosive substances and the latter by liquefied cryogenic gases, hot molten substances, or flames.
Choking agents	Substances that cause physical injury to the lungs. Exposure is through inhalation. In extreme cases, membranes swell and lungs become filled with liquid (pulmonary edema). Death results from lack of oxygen; hence, the victim is "choked". Phosgene (CG) is a choking agent. **Symptoms:** irritation to eyes/nose/throat, respiratory distress, nausea and vomiting, burning of exposed skin.
CO_2	Carbon dioxide gas.
Cold zone	Area where the command post and support functions that are necessary to control the incident are located. This is also referred to as the clean zone, green zone or support zone in other documents. (EPA Standard Operating Safety Guidelines, OSHA 29 CFR 1910.120, NFPA 472)

Page 358

1. A useful acronym to help remember your initial response actions is SIN. The acronym stands for _______, _________, and ___________.

2. When approaching the scene, you should attempt to identify the hazard from as far away as possible, using _________ if available.

3. If the responder at the scene of a transportation accident sees a placarded vehicle but does not know what material is represented by the placard, what section of the ERG should be consulted?
   a) The yellow section
   b) The green section
   c) The initial white section
   d) The orange guide pages

4. Which section of the ERG lists, in numerical order, UN Identification Numbers?
   a) The yellow section
   b) The green section
   c) The initial white section
   d) The orange guide pages

5. The ______ section of the ERG contains the guides to handling each material.

6. The guides for radioactive material recommend an initial isolation of ___ feet in all directions.

7. According to the ERG, _______ ________ should always take priority over radiological concerns at a radioactive material incident.

ANSWERS

1. safety
   isolation
   notification
2. binoculars
3. c
4. a
5. orange
6. 75
7. medical
   problems

INTRODUCTION

This module provides information about identifying packagings used to transport radioactive material and how to recognize this material when responding to a transportation incident.

Four types of packages will be discussed; Excepted packaging, Industrial packaging, Type A packaging and Type B packaging. Consideration for the mode of transporting radioactive material will be discussed.   You will learn the philosophy behind radioactive material packaging design as well as the safety features associated with the radioactive material package and the stringent package testing requirements.

PURPOSE

The purpose of this module is to provide you with a basic understanding of the types of packages used to transport radioactive material and the potential hazard posed by the material contained within these packages. This information will help increase your knowledge of appropriate responses to a radiological transportation incident.

MODULE OBJECTIVES

Upon completion of this module, you will be able to:

1. Identify typical packages used in the transport of radioactive material.
2. List examples of radioactive material that are shipped in various shipping packages.
3. Identify the risks associated with the various shipping packages.
4. Identify the testing methods for Type A and B Packages.

TRANSPORTING RADIOACTIVE MATERIAL

Radioactive materials are a vital part of our modern society. They are used in our hospitals, factories, laboratories and homes. Life would be more difficult if we had to stop using radioactive material. Many of the benefits we get from radioactive material cannot be obtained by any other means.

Doctors use them to diagnose and treat many diseases. Smoke detectors use a small amount of radioactive material to provide early warning of fires in our homes. Products like plastic wrap, radial tires, and coffee filters are manufactured in factories that use radioactive material. There are many more uses of radioactive materials in our modern society that provide enormous benefits.

Radioactive material is transported every day by highway, rail, air, and water. Radioactive material must be shipped from where it is produced to where it is used. The use of radioactive material sometimes produces radioactive waste that must then be shipped to a disposal site. Radioactive materials are transported according to very strict federal regulations. The regulations are designed to protect the public and the environment from risks associated with radioactive material during normal and accident conditions. The DOE complies with all applicable regulations pertaining to the transport of radioactive material.

Radioactive material is generally shipped in its most stable form. Typically, that means they are shipped as solids. When radioactive liquids or gases are transported, federal regulations require additional precautions. Careful research and design goes into packaging radioactive materials. Emergency planning, driver training, and strict government inspections are a part of a program that has **never** resulted in a radiologically related death or injury from a transportation incident.

HAZARD EVALUATION

Federal regulations place strict administrative controls on the transport of radioactive material. The worldwide philosophy of radioactive material transport is that:

- Safety should be primarily focused on the package. Packaging is the first line of defense.
- Package integrity should be directly related to the degree of hazard of the material it contains.

This two-part philosophy means that small quantities of radioactive material—quantities that would present little hazard if released— may be shipped in less secure packages than those that contain higher levels of radioactive material.

RADIOACTIVE MATERIAL PACKAGING

Radioactive material, like other commodities, is transported every day by highway, rail, air, and water. Radioactive material is packaged to ensure that radiation levels at the package surface do not exceed federal regulations. This ensures that shippers, the public, and the environment are not exposed to radiation levels that exceed recognized safe limits.

Different shipping packagings are required for various types, forms, quantities, and levels of radioactivity. We will discuss four packaging types:

- Excepted Packaging
- Industrial Packaging
- Type A Packaging
- Type B Packaging

Excepted Packaging is used to transport material with extremely low levels of radioactivity. Excepted packagings are authorized for limited quantities of radioactive material that would pose a very low hazard if released in an accident. Examples of material typically shipped in excepted packaging include consumer goods such as smoke detectors. Excepted packagings are excepted (excluded) from specific packaging, labeling, and shipping paper requirements; they are however, required to have the letters "UN" and the appropriate four-digit UN identification number marked on the outside of the package. Requirements for excepted packaging are addressed in 49 CFR 173.421.

Industrial Packaging is used in certain shipments of low activity material and contaminated objects, which are usually categorized as radioactive waste. Most low-level radioactive waste is shipped in these packages. Department of Transportation (DOT) regulations require that these packages allow no identifiable release of the material to the environment during normal transportation and handling. There are three categories of industrial packages: IP-1, IP-2, and IP-3. The category of package will be marked on the exterior of the package as shown below. Requirements for industrial packaging are addressed in 49 CFR 173.411.

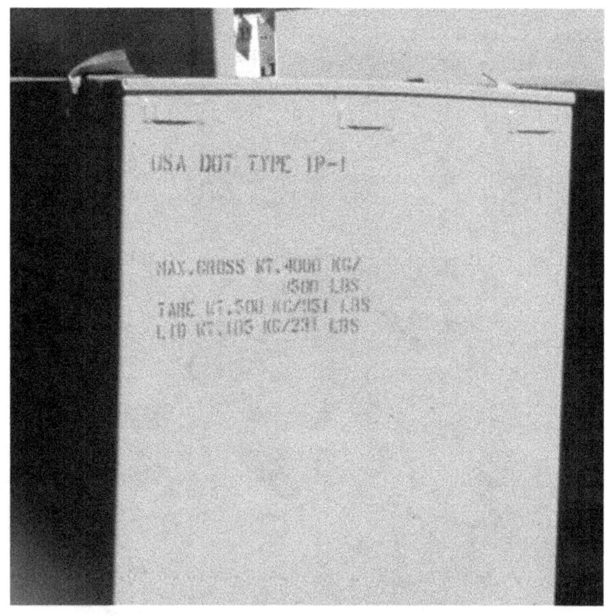

notes

Type A Packaging is used to transport small quantities of radioactive material with higher concentrations of radioactivity than those shipped in industrial packagings. They are typically constructed of steel, wood, or fiberboard, and have an inner containment vessel made of glass, plastic, or metal surrounded with packing material made of polyethylene, rubber, or vermiculite. Examples of material typically shipped in Type A Packages include nuclear medicines (radiopharmaceuticals), radioactive waste, and radioactive sources used in industrial applications. Type A packaging and its radioactive contents must meet standard testing requirements designed to ensure that the package retains its containment integrity and shielding under normal transport conditions.   Requirements for Type A packaging are addressed in 49 CFR 173.412.

Type A Packages must withstand moderate degrees of heat, cold, reduced air pressure, vibration, impact, water spray, drop, penetration, and stacking tests. Type A Packages are not, however, designed to withstand the forces of an accident. The consequences of a release of the material in one of these packages would not be significant since the quantity of material in this package is so limited. Type A packagings are only used to transport non life-endangering amounts of radioactive material.

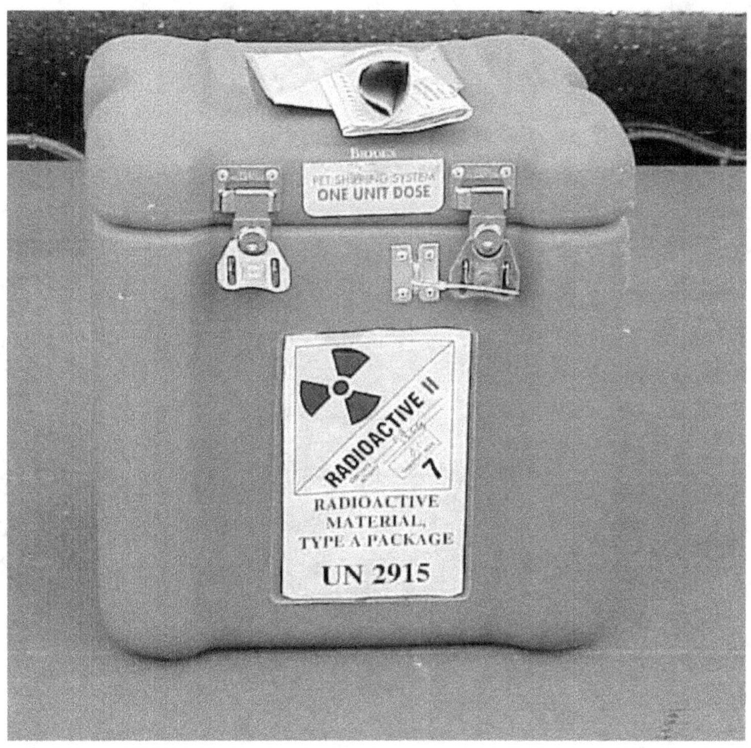

M E R R T T
Radioactive Material Shipping Packages

Type B Packaging is designed to transport material with the highest levels of radioactivity. As illustrated in the photos below, Type B packagings range from small hand-held radiography cameras to heavily shielded steel casks that weigh up to 125 tons. Examples of material transported in Type B packagings include spent nuclear fuel, high-level radioactive waste, and high concentrations of other radioactive material such as cesium and cobalt. These package designs must withstand all Type A tests, and a series of tests that simulate severe or "worst-case" accident conditions. Accident conditions are simulated by performance testing and engineering analysis. Life-endangering amounts of radioactive material are required to be transported in Type B Packages. Requirements for Type B packaging are addressed in 49 CFR 173.411. 49 CFR 173.413 and 10 CFR 71.

notes

To demonstrate that Type B Packages can withstand a severe accident, a tractor-trailer (below) carrying a Type B Package prototype was crashed into a massive concrete wall at 84 miles per hour. The package was slightly dented, but it did not release its simulated radioactive material.

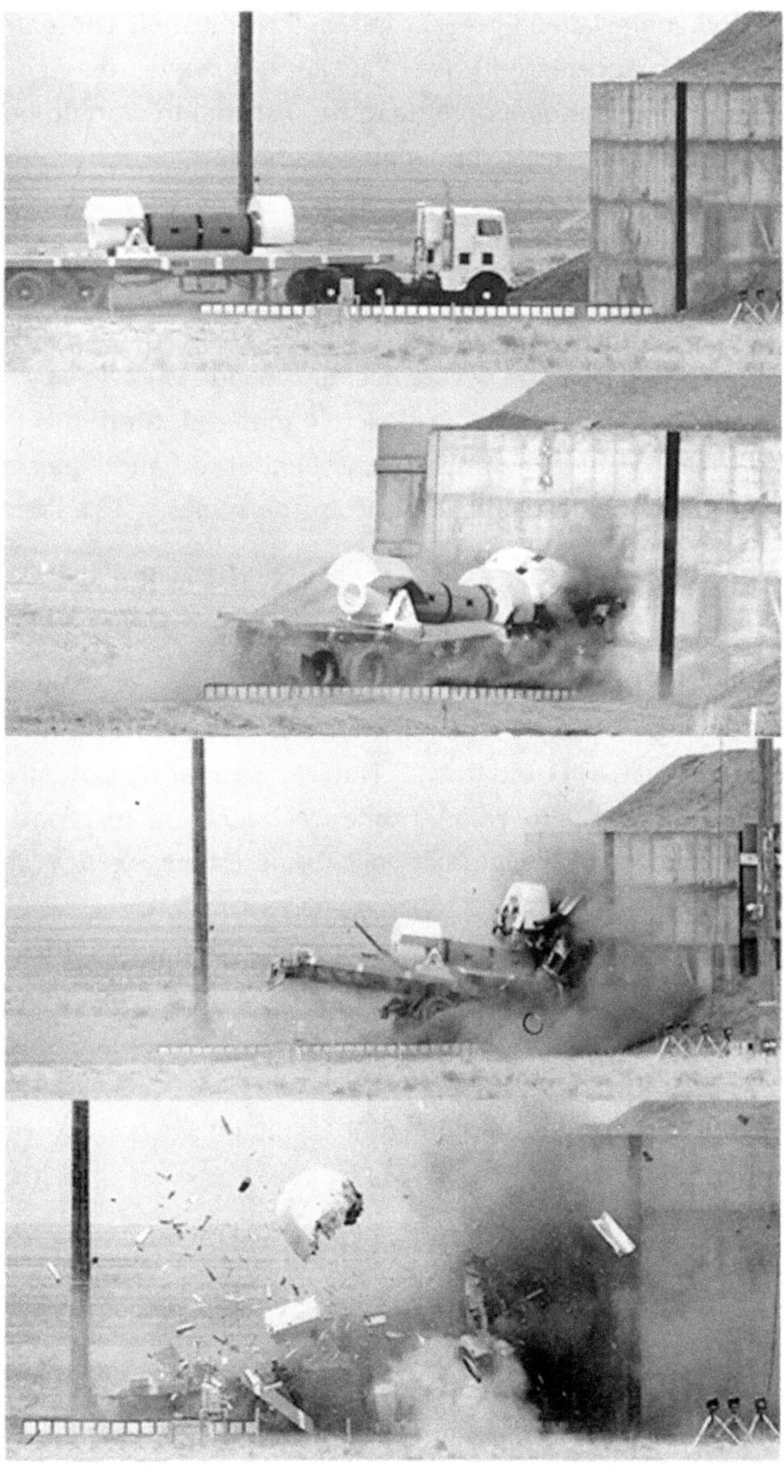

M E R R T T
Radioactive Material Shipping Packages

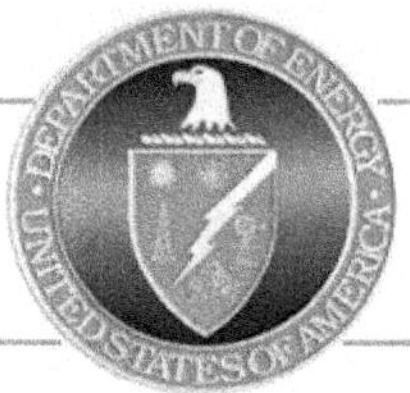

RISKS ASSOCIATED WITH SHIPPING PACKAGES

Unlike other hazard classes, radioactive material in transport has additional information about potential risk(s) to the responder. Some of this information can be obtained by first identifying the packaging type for the material being shipped. Excepted, Industrial, and Type A Packages contain non life-endangering amounts of radioactive material and present minimal risk if their contents are released in an accident. Type B Packages, however, may contain life-endangering amounts of radioactive material that could pose a significant risk if released during an accident.

The philosophy behind radioactive material transportation—where safety is primarily focused on packaging and package integrity being appropriate to the material hazard—dictates that Type B Packages be designed to withstand severe accident conditions. In DOE's 50-year history of transporting radioactive material, there has never been a release from a Type B Package. In addition, there has never been an injury or death resulting from the release of radioactive material in a transportation incident.

RADIOACTIVE MATERIAL PACKAGE TESTING

Two federal agencies regulate the testing of radioactive material package designs for use in the United States: the U.S. Department of Transportation (DOT) and the U.S. Nuclear Regulatory Commission (NRC). DOT and NRC regulations are based on international regulations issued by the International Atomic Energy Agency (IAEA).

The DOT is responsible for specifying required test conditions for most packages. The NRC certifies that packages designed for material with higher levels of radioactivity (i.e., Type B Packages), such as spent fuel, meet NRC test requirements. Package designs are tested using computer simulation, scale model testing, and/or full-scale testing.

notes

PACKAGE TESTING REQUIREMENTS

Type A Tests

Type A Packages must be able to withstand a series of tests that simulate normal transport conditions. These tests include:

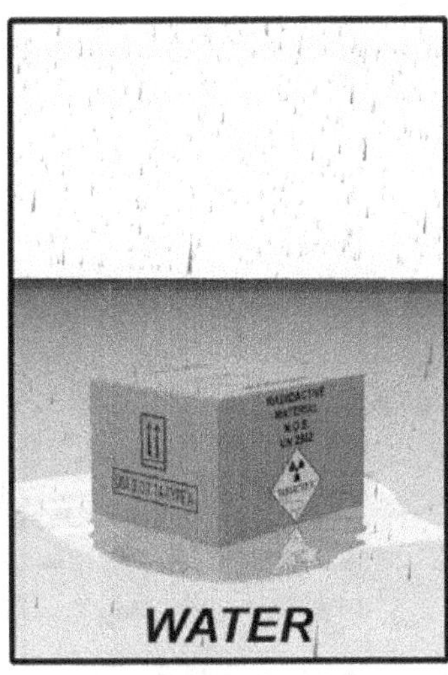

Water spray for 1 hour to simulate rainfall of 2 inches per hour.

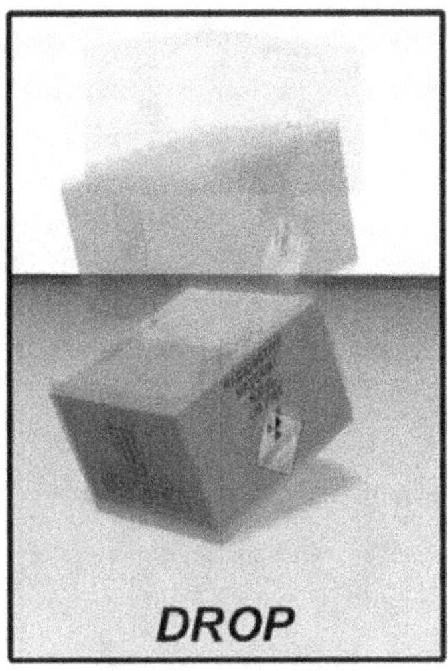

Free drop test onto a flat, hard surface.

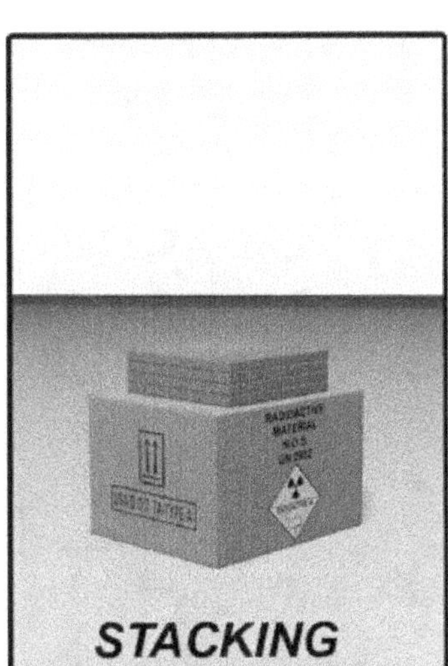

Stacking test of at least 5 times the weight of the package. This test is conducted for at least 24 hours.

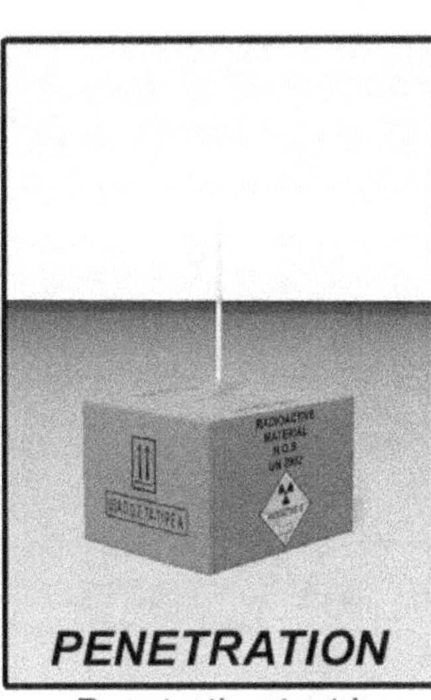

Penetration test by dropping a 13-pound, 1.25-inch diameter bar vertically onto the package from a height of 3.3 feet.

PACKAGE TESTING REQUIREMENTS

Type B Tests

In addition to the requirements for Type A Packages, the Nuclear Regulatory Commission (NRC) requires that Type B Packages be able to withstand a series of tests that simulate severe accident conditions. These tests are conducted sequentially and include:

FREE DROP

A 30-foot free drop onto a flat, essentially unyielding surface so that the package's weakest point is struck

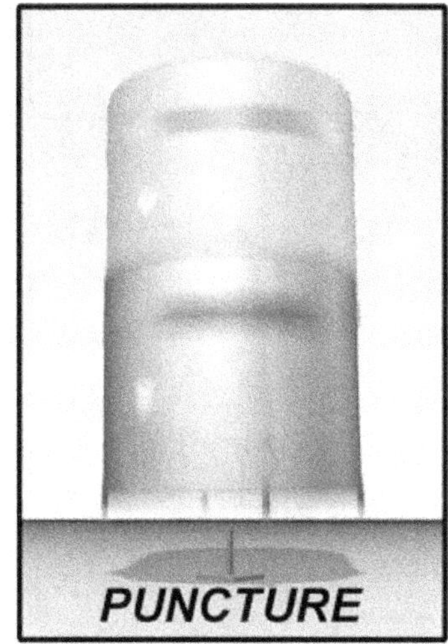

PUNCTURE

A 40-inch free drop onto a 6-inch diameter steel rod at least 8 inches long, striking the package at its most vulnerable spot.

THERMAL

Exposure of the entire package to 1475°F for 30 minutes.

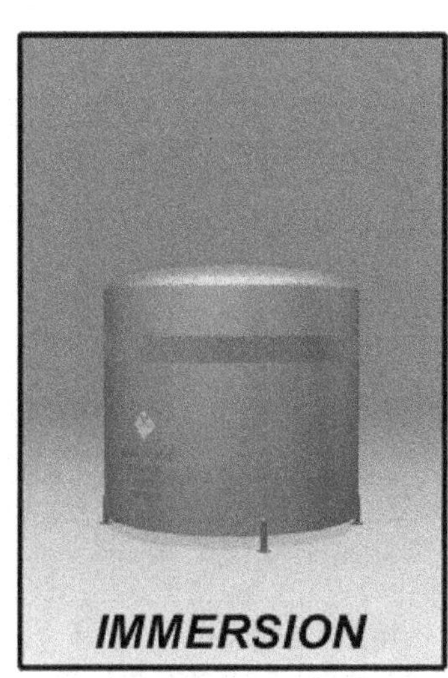

IMMERSION

Immersion of the package under 50 feet of water for at least 8 hours.

1. This type of packaging, along with its radioactive contents, must meet standard testing requirements designed to ensure that the package retains its containment integrity and shielding under normal transport conditions.
   a) Type A packaging
   b) Type B packaging
   c) Industrial packaging
   d) Excepted packaging

2. _______ packaging must be able to withstand a series of tests that simulate severe or "worst case" accident conditions.

3. Radiopharmaceuticals are typically shipped in _______ packagings and spent nuclear fuel is typically shipped in _______ packagings.

4. Which of the following statements best applies to the risks associated with material shipped in Type A Packages?
   a) Type A Packages are used to transport very high levels of radioactive material.
   b) Type A Packages are used to transport exempt quantities of radioactive material.
   c) Type A Packages are built to withstand the most severe accident conditions.
   d) Type A Packages contain non life-endangering amounts of radioactive material.

ANSWERS

1. a
2. Type B
3. Type A
   Type B
4. d

M E R R T T

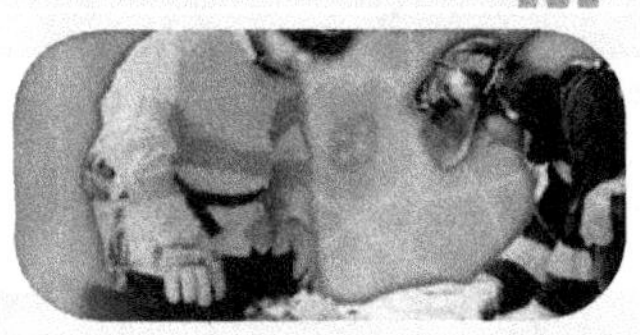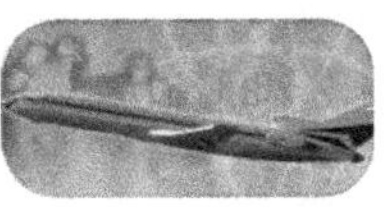

M E R R T T
Patient Handling

INTRODUCTION

This module provides information on how to assess the risk of your response efforts, remembering that the care of the patient takes priority over radiological concerns.

The three general classes of patients (exposed to radiation, externally contaminated, internally contaminated) encountered at a radioactive material transportation incident will be discussed as well as proper procedures for safely rescuing and handling patients at the scene.

PURPOSE

The purpose of this module is to help you assess the potential risks in handling contaminated patients at a radioactive material transportation incident. This module will aid you in preparing patients for transport from the incident scene to the hospital.

MODULE OBJECTIVES

Upon completion of this module, you will be able to:

1. Identify the risks to response personnel when rescuing injured persons at a radioactive material transportation incident.
2. Identify the importance of gross decontamination for radiologically contaminated patients.
3. Identify methods for preparing radiologically contaminated patients for transport to the hospital.

ASSESSING THE RISK

At the site of a radiological transportation incident, it is as important to ensure your own safety as it is to ensure the safety of all patients at the scene. Always approach an incident site with caution and look for all hazards. Isolate the area and keep non-essential people away from the scene and outside the safety perimeter. **When handling patients, use Universal Precautions as an approach to infection control** (per 29 CFR 1910.1030).

Questions to consider before entering the incident scene include:

- How much and what type of protection does your personal protective equipment (PPE) provide?
- How much time will it take and what is the best route to rescue patient(s) and avoid radiation or contamination areas? (Planning a strategy before entering the scene may help reduce the time spent near radiation sources).
- What other hazards are present (fire, spilled diesel, downed power lines, etc.)?

Remember that care for the patient takes priority over radiological hazard assessment. Look for the following when entering the area to perform rescue operations:

- How many (if any) patients?
- What types of injuries?
- Are there any packages with visible labels?
- Do any packages look as though they are leaking, or breached?
  Remember that dose rates from undamaged packages are considered to have acceptable radiation/contamination levels on the surface of the package.
- What types of packages are present?
  Remember that Excepted, Industrial, and Type A Packages contain non-life-endangering amounts of radioactive material.

M E R R T T
Patient Handling

EMERGENCY MEDICAL PROCEDURES

Medical problems take priority over radiological concerns. Use of Universal Precautions will help reduce the spread of radiological contamination. Radiation exposure or contamination resulting from a radioactive material shipment will not cause unconsciousness or immediate visible signs of injury.

Some radioactive materials are corrosive (e.g., uranium hexafluoride - UF6), and contact with corrosives may result in chemical burns or respiratory injury. Chemical burns from corrosive radioactive material are managed like any other corrosive injury. Treat patients according to the nature of their injuries. The presence of radiation will not interfere with any rescue or extrication equipment used, nor will it influence the extinguishing properties of fire fighting agents.

Unless your standard operating procedures dictate otherwise, do not delay treatment due to the lack of survey meters or protective clothing. According to the ERG, emergency life-saving assistance is always of higher priority than the priority for measuring radiation levels. Take precautions against the spread of contamination. When handling a potentially contaminated patient, a calm attitude may be the most important form of treatment you can provide.

Remember that radiation exposure is different from contamination. Contamination is a material—something that you can get on you or in you. Radiation (exposure), however, is energy—something that can pass right through you—and exposure to radiation alone will not contaminate you.

DOE offers a Transportation Emergency Preparedness Program (TEPP) model procedure for packaging and transporting contaminated patients as well as a model procedure for medical examiners/coroners on handling potentially contaminated human remains.[1]

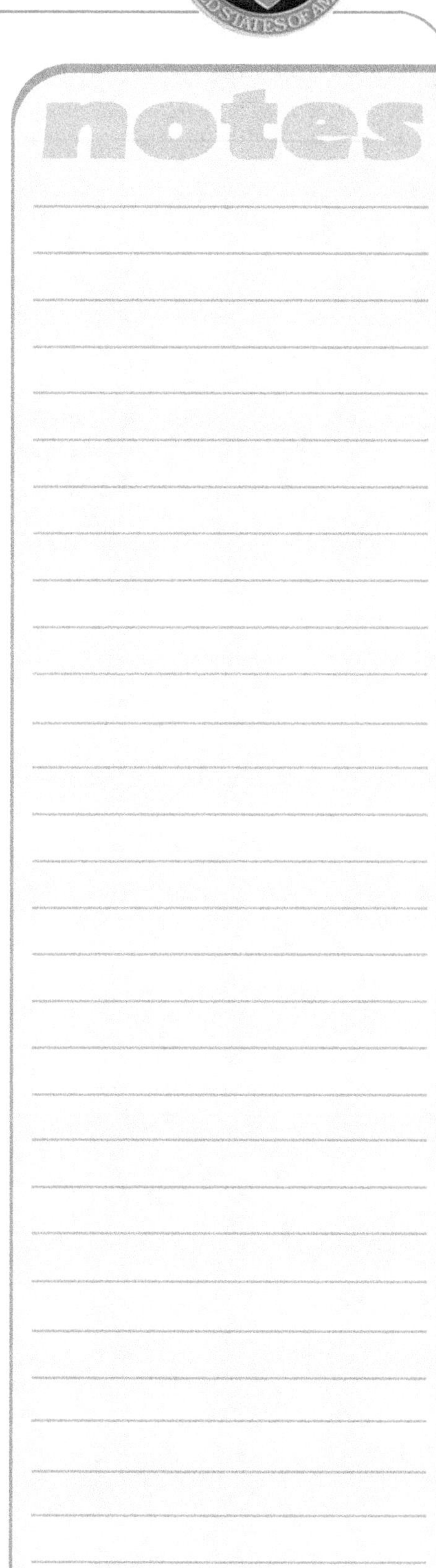

---

[1] Information can be obtained at the Department of Energy's web site: http://web.em.doe.gov/otem/program.html.

TYPES OF EXPOSURE

In a radiation incident, you may encounter three general classes of patients who may be classified under one or more of the conditions listed below: *Please note that a patient may experience **a combination** of any of these conditions.*

1. **Patient was exposed to radiation from an external source**

   A patient exposed to radiation alone will not pose a contamination problem. The degree of radiation-induced injury depends on the radiation dose the patient received. Following external exposure, a patient is not radioactive or contaminated and can be handled without fear or concern of spreading contamination to you or the environment.

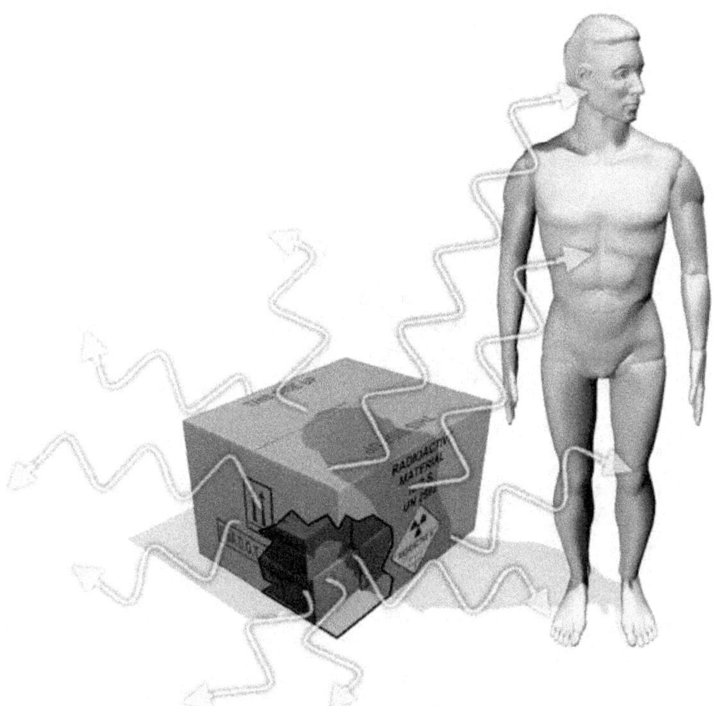

   Treat a patient exposed to external radiation no differently than a person who may have received radiation therapy. If the level of exposure was low, the patient may be viewed as someone who received diagnostic X-rays. If the level of exposure is very high, subsequent treatment at a specialized hospital may be necessary. It is important to remember, however, that no one has ever received a medically significant exposure to radiation during a transportation incident involving radioactive material.

2. Externally contaminated patient

Coming into contact with radioactive material (gas, liquid, or solid) that has been released into the environment can contaminate a patient. Externally contaminated patients may have radioactive material on portions of their bodies or clothing. This contamination, if spread, presents a potential hazard to a hospital environment and to other people. If you suspect external contamination and the patient is seriously injured, give lifesaving assistance immediately. Contaminated patients should be handled with protocols (i.e., Universal Precautions) similar to those used for bloodborne pathogens.

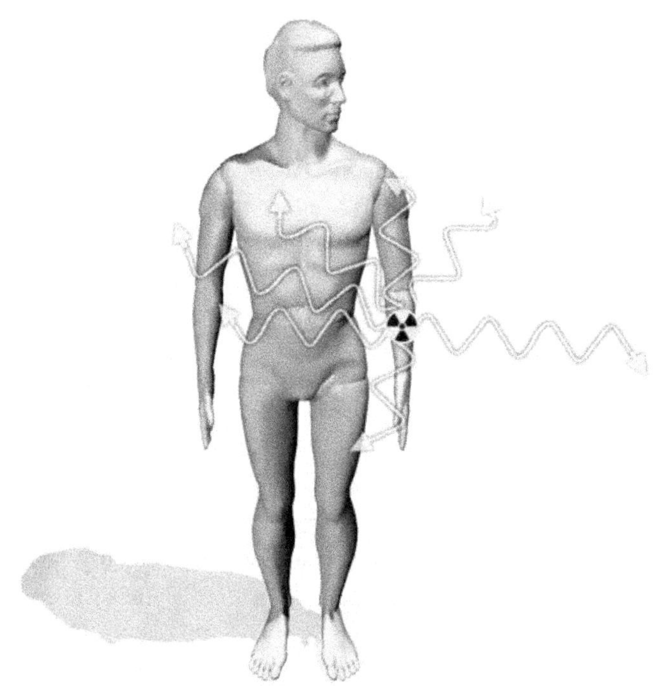

Wear protective clothing (coveralls, gloves, turnout gear, etc.) while handling an externally contaminated patient. This will limit the spread the contamination. You should wrap the patient in a blanket or sheet during movement, and save all related clothing and bedding in plastic bags. Identify the bags clearly as "RADIOACTIVE - DO NOT DISCARD." The outer clothing of response personnel attending to the patient also needs to be saved and surveyed by qualified personnel for contamination. Contaminated items will have to be handled and disposed of in accordance with state and federal regulations.

A patient could have contamination in, or near, a wound. In this case, your primary objective must be to treat the wound and prevent any further spread of radioactive contamination into it. An open cut or wound can allow contamination to enter the body, causing internal contamination.

3. Internally contaminated patient

Internally contaminated patients present minimal risk to response personnel. A patient can become internally contaminated if radioactive material is inhaled, ingested, or introduced to the body through a cut or wound.

The internally contaminated patient may also be externally contaminated and, if so, must be treated using the procedures described earlier. The internally contaminated patient will require specialized treatment at a hospital to prevent further uptake of the contaminant and/or to promote its removal from the body.

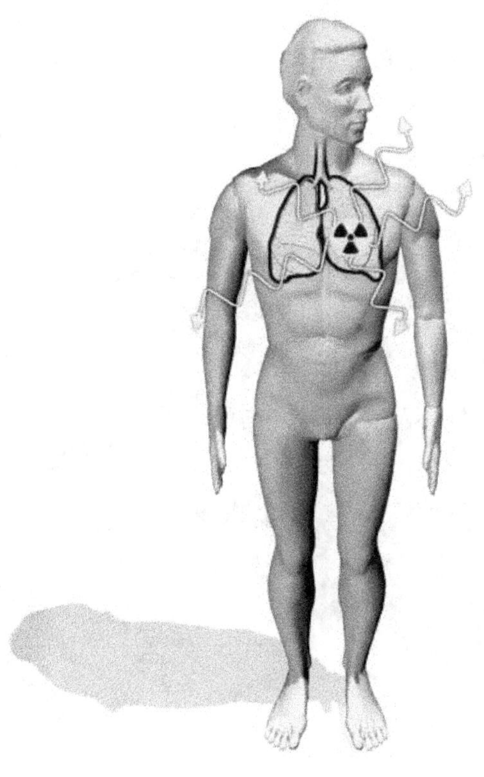

M E R R T T
Patient Handling

PATIENT HANDLING/GROSS DECONTAMINATION

If you suspect contamination (presence of damaged or leaking packages), removing all of a patient's outer clothing—a process called gross decontamination (decon)—can dramatically reduce the amount of contaminants on the body. The best technique for gross decontamination is to cut the patient's outer clothing up the middle and carefully lay the cut clothing open, away from the patient. This process minimizes the spread of contamination. A gross decon should only be considered if radioactive material packages appear breached and you suspect that contamination has been released.

If you suspect contamination and have performed a gross decon, leave the patient's clothing inside the hot zone[2]. This clothing will need to be bagged and identified as radioactive. Minimizing the amount/quantity of contaminated or radioactive material (removed clothing, packages, etc.) in the treatment area will help keep radiation dose rates low. If possible, wipe any exposed surfaces— especially those around the patient's mouth, if you are applying an oxygen mask or respirator. Additional decontamination should only be attempted by personnel trained in radiological decontamination (e.g., Radiation Authority) and only if time permits.

---

[2] Hot zone refers to the area surrounding the incident site where contamination is suspected. This area may also be referred to as the exclusion zone or control zone.

The following step-by-step procedure is provided as an example, and can be used as a guideline, for performing gross decon and proper packaging of a potentially contaminated patient.

1. Utilize the ERG to conduct a scene size-up. Establish contamination control zones and, without entering the hot zone, determine essential treatment equipment needed.

   Note: If Incident Command has already been established, EMS care providers should report to the Incident Commander for a scene size-up. If response actions are being initiated by EMS care providers and the scene size-up has been completed, care providers should also consider reducing the possibility of contamination spread by only carrying essential medical equipment inside the hot zone.

2. Prior to entry into the hot zone, prepare the backboard or other device that will be used to remove the patient from the hot zone as follows:

   A. Spread a protective barrier (blanket, sheet, etc.).

   B. Spread a second protective barrier (blanket, sheet, etc.).

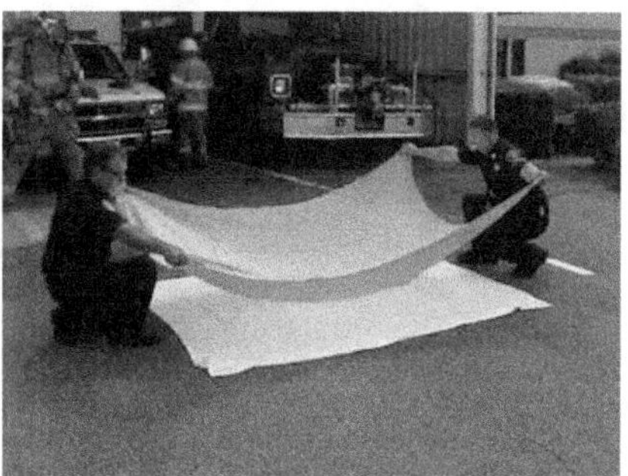

C. Place the backboard or other device in the center of the protective barrier.

D. Roll edges of the protective barrier until only the remaining unrolled portion can be placed on top of the backboard or other extrication device.

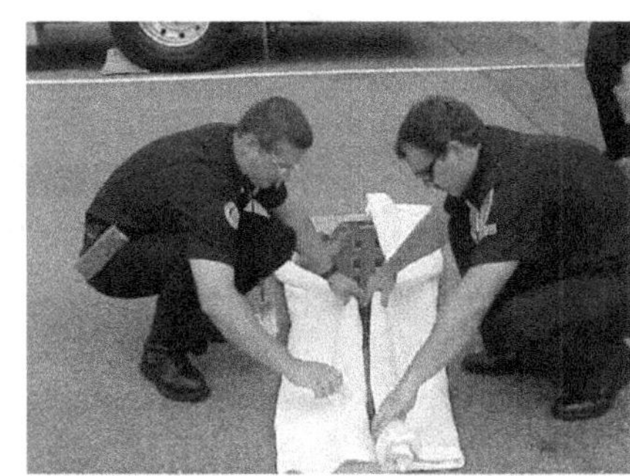

E. Place essential medical response equipment on top of the backboard or other device. Avoid taking advanced life support equipment into the hot zone.

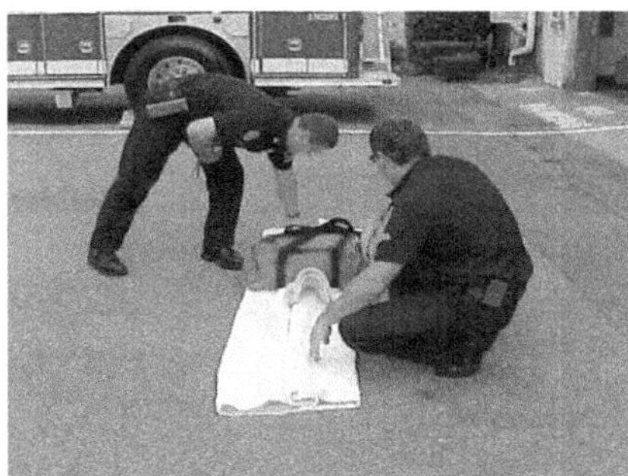

3. Don appropriate protective clothing. Firefighting gear or Body Substance Isolation Clothing (BSIC) is recommended, including 2 pair of latex gloves and respiratory protection if available (such as Self-Contained Breathing Apparatus, Air Purifying Respirator, or N95 Particulate Mask).

M E R R T T
Patient Handling

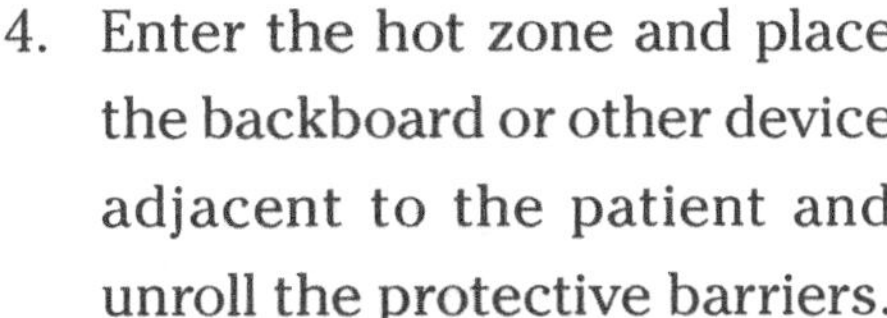

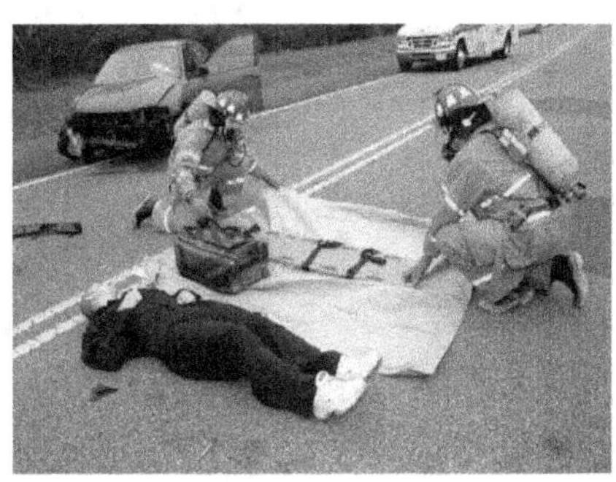

4. Enter the hot zone and place the backboard or other device adjacent to the patient and unroll the protective barriers.

   Note: The double blanket method will help reduce the possibility of spreading contamination. The outer blanket will reduce/eliminate responder contact with contaminated surfaces and protect the backboard or other device from contamination. EMS equipment should be placed on the blanket to minimize the potential for equipment to become contaminated. The inner blanket, when wrapped around the patient, will encapsulate any remaining radioactive contamination to the patient.

   Life threatening injuries such as severe hemorrhage and airway control should be corrected immediately. Advanced life support should not be attempted in the hot zone. The patient should be promptly packaged and transferred to the clean area for further care.

5. Evaluate the need for reducing contamination on the patient.

   Note: Contamination reduction should be considered if the incident/ accident scene contains open or breached radioactive material packages.

6. Reduce contamination by very carefully cutting the patients clothing away from the body.

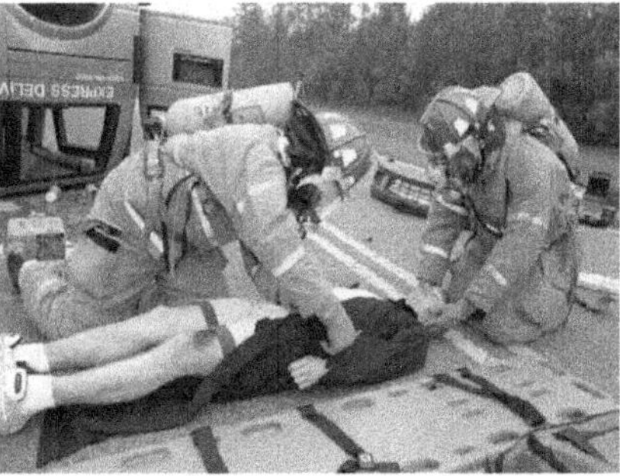

   Note: Cut clothing on the center of all body extremities and the trunk. Carefully lay cut clothing open, exposing the patient's body.

7. Responders should carefully remove their outer pair of latex gloves.

8. Treat non-life-threatening injuries as necessary. If contamination is suspected in or near a wound/injury, the primary option is to treat the wound/injury and prevent additional spread of contamination.

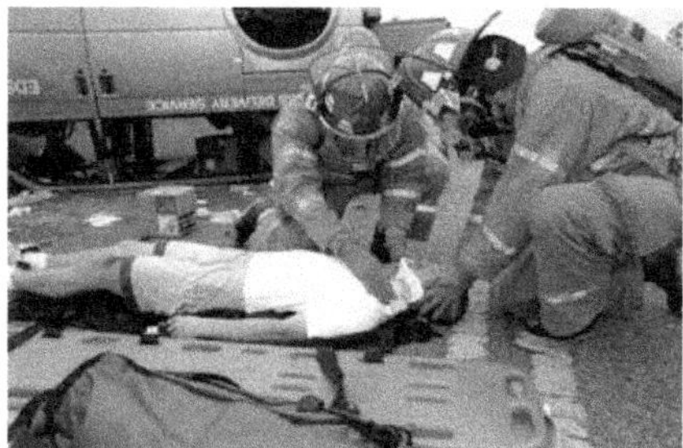

Note: If cleaning of injured area is to be conducted, wipe away from all open wounds or the airway. Only use the wipe(s) one time and handle all waste as potentially contaminated material. Place the wipe(s) in a controlled disposal container so that they can be monitored for radiological contamination by the local radiation authority.

9. Load the patient on to the backboard or other device using standard medical protocols and wrap the inner protective barrier around the patient.

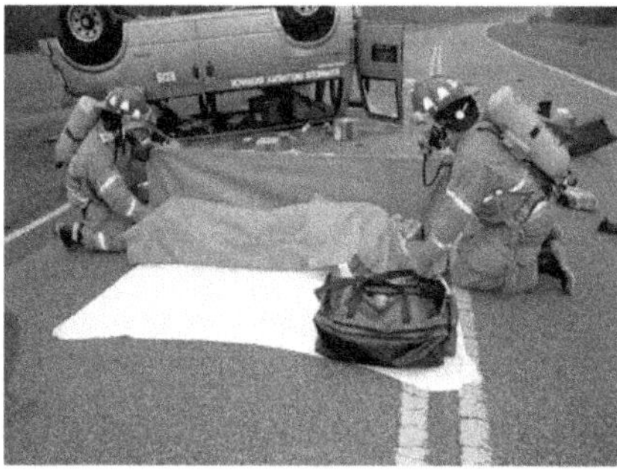

Note: All clothing removed from patient, gloves, and outer blanket should remain inside the hot zone. These items should be handled as radioactive waste. The local radiation authority will coordinate the packaging and removal of waste.

notes

10. Emergency medical care providers should hand carry the patient to the boundary of the hot zone.

11. A second team of care providers should have an appropriate transportation device waiting at the boundary of the hot zone. This device should also be covered with a protective barrier.

12. At the boundary of the hot zone, responders should pass the patient across the control line to waiting responders.

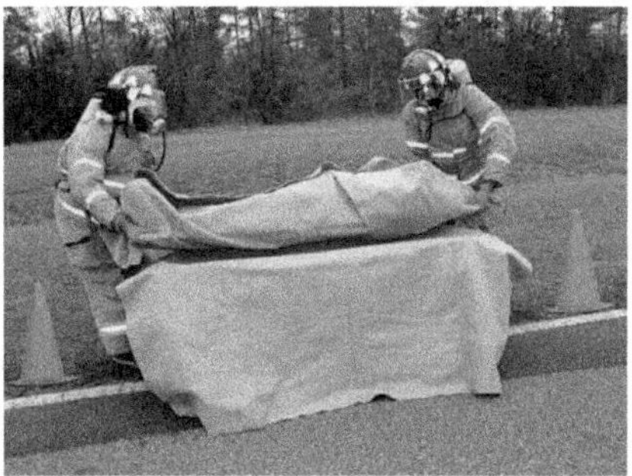

Note: Care providers within the hot zone should remain there until surveyed by the local radiation authority or other qualified person and determined to be free of contamination. If additional responders are not available, the treating responders should remove protective clothing at the hot zone boundary and provide transportation of the patient to the appropriate medical facility. Based on local procedures, the patient may require additional transfers at each of the contamination control zone lines.

13. After transferring the patient to the clean area, emergency medical care providers should cover the patient with the protective barrier that was placed over the transport device.

14. Load the patient into the ambulance for transport to the hospital. EMS care providers inside the ambulance should wear appropriate protective clothing.

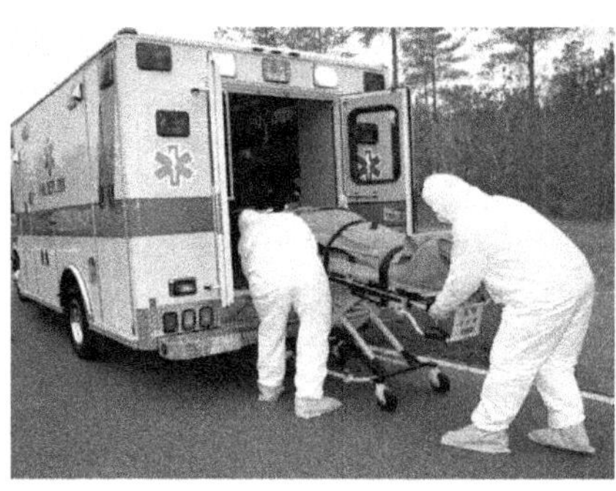

Note: To reduce/prevent possible contamination of the ambulance, consider the following additional precautions: open the protective barrier covering the patient only to administer necessary patient treatment (e.g., introduction of IV fluids, etc.); place floor covering (paper or plastic, etc.) on ambulance floor; avoid opening ambulance cabinets—work out of portable response kits as much as possible; and, consider all items used in the treatment of the patient potentially contaminated. Consider turning off the ambulance's patient compartment ventilation system to avoid spreading airborne contamination outside the ambulance.

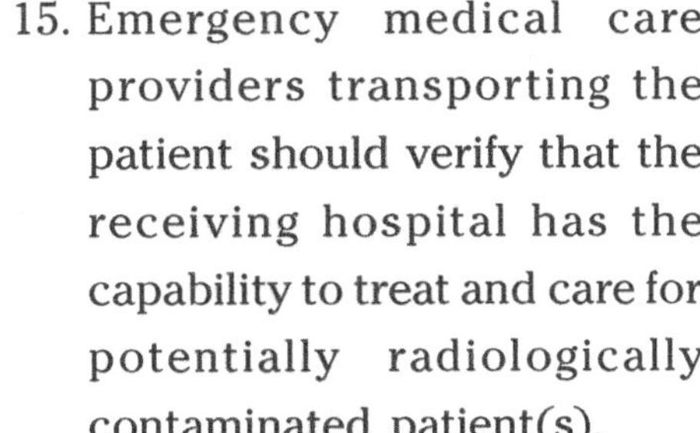

M E R R T T
Patient Handling

15. Emergency medical care providers transporting the patient should verify that the receiving hospital has the capability to treat and care for potentially radiologically contaminated patient(s).

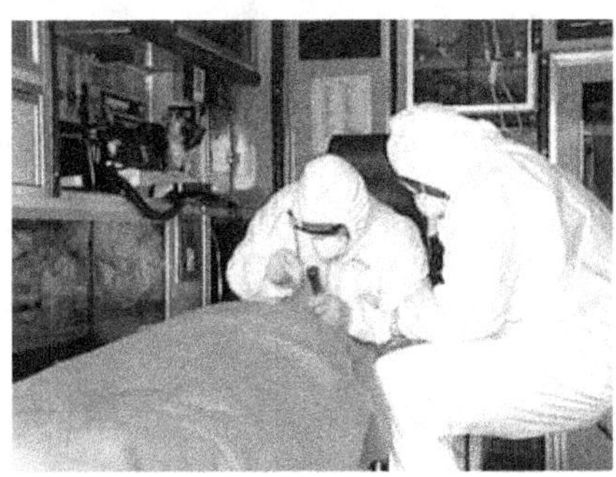

16. Upon confirmation, emergency medical care providers should notify the receiving hospital of patient status, radiological contamination concerns, estimated time of arrival, and the need for the monitoring of themselves and the ambulance. Ask whether the hospital has any special instructions or procedures for receiving contaminated patients. The hospital, for example, may have a special entrance for radiologically contaminated patients.

17. Emergency medical care providers, upon arrival at the hospital, should follow the hospital's radiological control protocol. At the minimum, emergency medical care providers should remove the patient from the ambulance and then establish a contamination control zone in and around the ambulance. The ambulance should not be returned to regular service until the crew, vehicle, and equipment have been surveyed for radiological contamination.

18. Do not eat, drink, smoke, or chew until you have been surveyed and released by the Radiation Safety Officer at the hospital or other qualified radiation authority.

Check Your Understanding

1. At the scene of a transportation incident, it is important to approach the site with caution looking for all __________.

2. Some radioactive materials are __________ and may cause chemical burns.

3. Treatment protocols at a radioactive material transportation incident should be based on which of the following:
   a) Treat for radiation exposure first
   b) Treat for contamination first
   c) Treat injuries and medical priorities first
   d) Withhold treatment until the patient is transported

4. In a radiation incident, you may encounter three general classes of patients. These, either singularly or in combination, are:
   1) ____
   2) ____
   3) ____

5. A patient who has been exposed to __________ alone presents no hazard to emergency care providers.

6. Performing a _____ _____ can dramatically reduce the amount of contaminants on a patient.

ANSWERS
1. hazards
2. corrosive
3. c
4. See pgs. 4 to 6
5. radiation
6. gross decon

M E R R T T
Radiological Terminology and Units

notes

INTRODUCTION

This module will provide you with information about four different types of ionizing radiation: alpha, beta, gamma, and neutron. Radiological terminology used in the transport of radioactive material and radioactive waste will be defined and discussed. This module also identifies the different units used for measuring radiation and radioactivity.

PURPOSE

The purpose of this module is to increase your knowledge of ionizing radiation. Knowing the terminology and measuring units associated with radioactive material will help you communicate more effectively with assisting agencies while responding to an incident involving radioactive material.

MODULE OBJECTIVES

Upon completion of this module, you will be able to:

1. Identify four basic types of ionizing radiation.
2. Identify the terms used to measure radiation and radioactivity.
3. Identify terminology and acronyms associated with shipments of radioactive material.
4. Identify commonly used Proper Shipping Names for radioactive material.

notes

THE FOUR BASIC TYPES OF IONIZING RADIATION

Most of the commonly transported radioactive materials emit one or more forms of ionizing radiation. The four basic types of ionizing radiation are alpha radiation, beta radiation, gamma radiation, and neutron radiation. All four types differ in their penetrating power and the manner in which they affect human tissue. To give you a general understanding of each type, they are discussed here.

Alpha

Alpha radiation consists of high-energy particles that are relatively large, heavy, and only travel a short distance. Because they are so large and heavy, alpha particles lose their energy very rapidly, have a low penetrating ability, and short range of travel—only a few inches in air. Because of the alpha particle's short range and limited penetrating ability, external shielding is not required. A few inches of air, a sheet of paper, or the dead (outer) layer of skin that surrounds our bodies easily stops alpha particles. Alpha radiation poses minimal biological hazard outside the body. The greatest hazard from alpha-emitting material occurs when the material is inhaled or ingested. Once inside the body, the alpha radiation can cause harm to individual cells or organs.

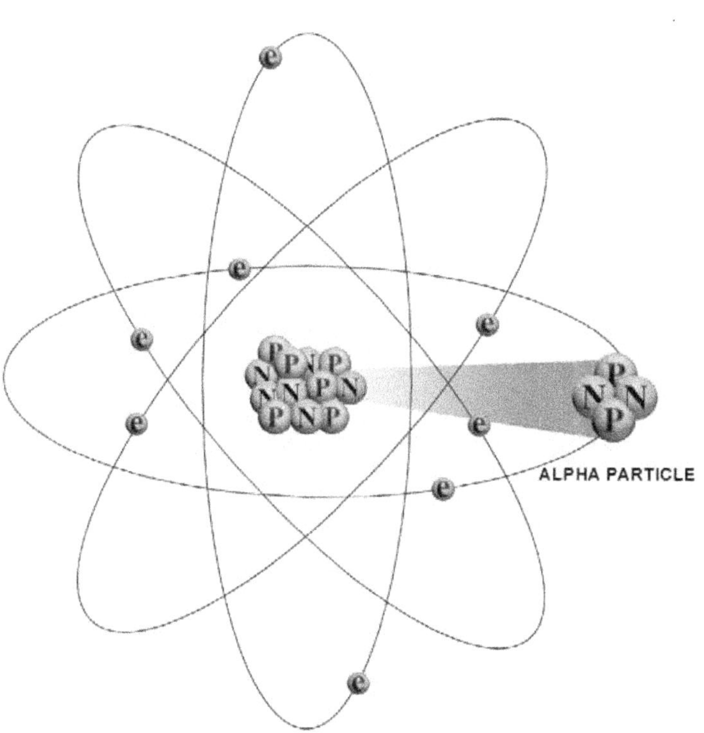

Beta

Beta radiation consists of particles that are smaller, lighter, and travel farther than alpha radiation. Because they are smaller and lighter, beta radiation is more penetrating than alpha radiation. The range of penetration in human tissue is less than ¼ inch. In air, beta radiation can travel several feet. Beta radiation may be blocked or shielded by plastic (SCBA face shield), aluminum, thick cardboard, several layers of clothing (bunker gear) or the walls of a building.

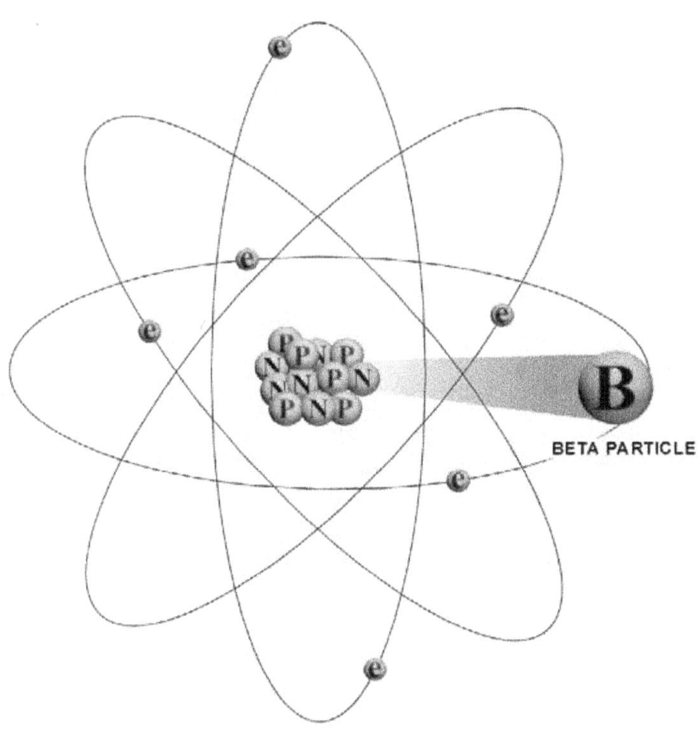

Outside the body, beta radiation constitutes only a slight hazard. Because beta radiation penetrates only a fraction of an inch into living skin tissue, it does not reach the major organs of the body. However, exposure to high levels of beta radiation can cause damage to the skin and eyes. Internally, beta radiation is less hazardous than alpha radiation because beta particles travel farther than alpha particles and, as a result, the energy deposited by the beta radiation is spread out over a larger area. This causes less harm to individual cells or organs.

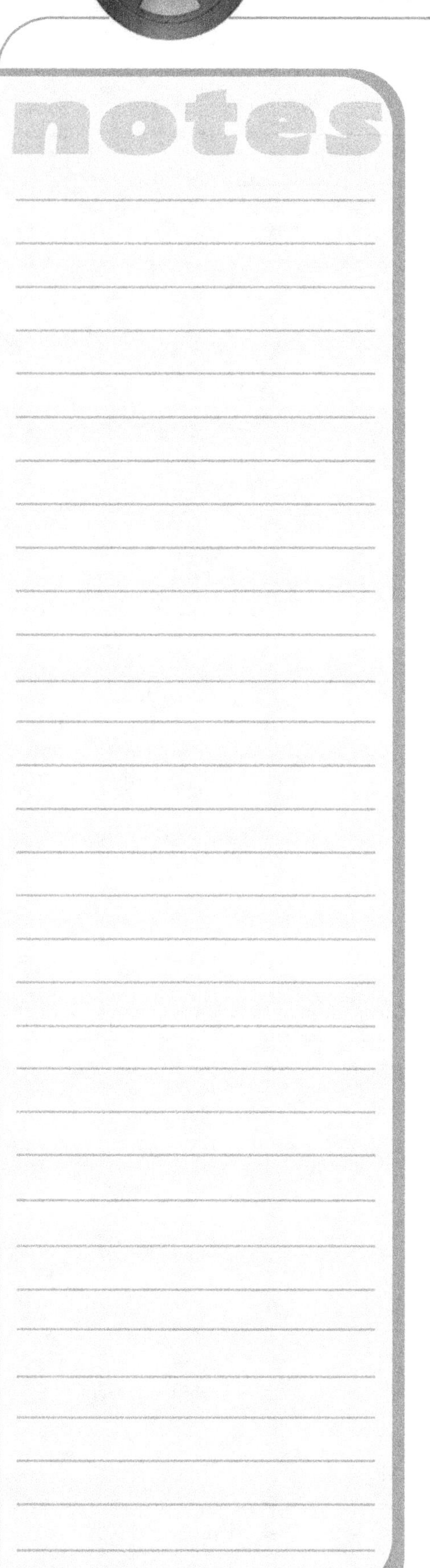

Gamma

Gamma radiation, like X-rays, is electromagnetic radiation. This means that it does not consist of particles like alpha and beta radiation but, rather, waves of energy that have no mass and no electrical charge. Because they have no mass and no electrical charge, they are able to travel great distances and require dense material as shielding. Gamma radiation poses a hazard to the entire body because it can easily penetrate human tissue. Lead, steel, and concrete are commonly used to shield gamma radiation.

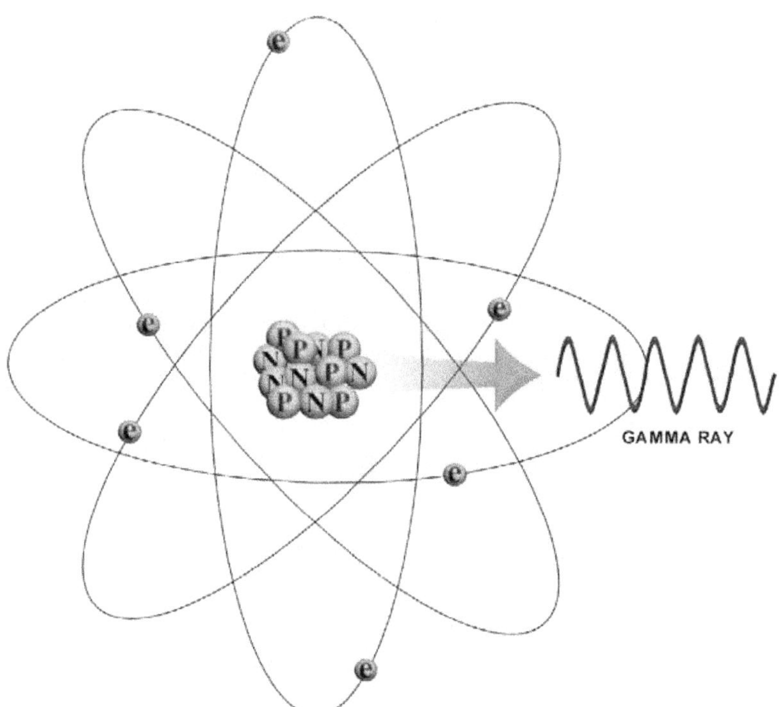

Neutron

Neutron radiation consists of neutron particles that are ejected from an atom's nucleus. Neutron radiation can travel great distances and is highly penetrating like gamma radiation. It is best shielded with high hydrogen content material (e.g., water, plastic). In transportation situations, neutron radiation is not commonly encountered.

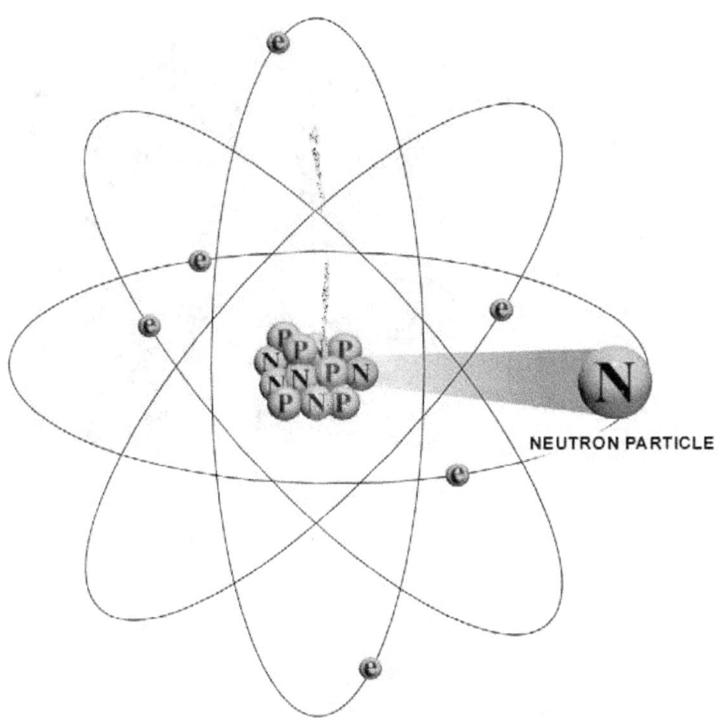

TERMINOLOGY ASSOCIATED WITH RADIOACTIVE MATERIAL SHIPMENTS

Familiarity with terminology used for describing radioactive material in transport will help you function and communicate more effectively during a transportation incident involving radioactive material. The following terms are often associated with radioactive material shipments. These terms can be seen as a part of a Proper Shipping Name (e.g., Radioactive Material, Type A package, fissile) and/or on shipping papers:

Fissile Material - material whose atoms are capable of nuclear fission (capable of being split). Department of Transportation (DOT) regulations define fissile material as plutonium-239, plutonium-241, uranium-233, uranium-

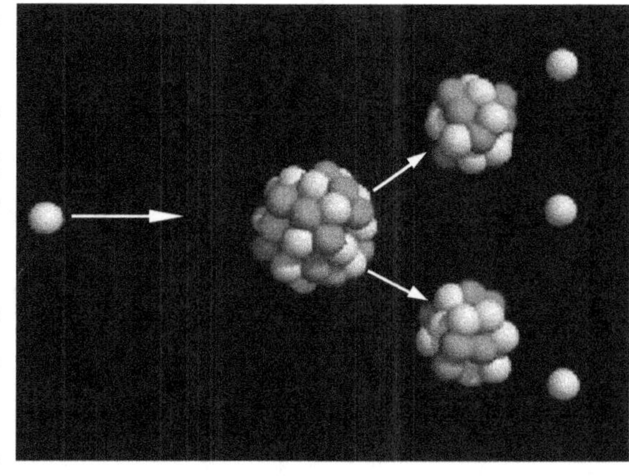

235, or any combination of these radionuclides. This material is usually transported with additional shipping controls that limit the quantity of material in any one shipment. Packages used for fissile material are designed and tested to prevent a fission reaction from occurring during normal transport conditions as well as hypothetical accident conditions.

Criticality Safety Index (CSI) - means a number which is used to provide control over the accumulation of packages, overpacks, or freight containers containing fissile material. The CSI is assigned by the shipper and is displayed on the FISSILE label. Under normal conditions, the aggregate criticality safety indices of all fissile material packages on a shipment will not exceed 50.

LSA - an acronym that stands for low specific activity. This means radioactive material with a limited amount of radioactivity in relationship to the total amount of material present. Material such as uranium and thorium ores, mill tailings, and contaminated earth are often transported as LSA material. Radioactive waste is commonly transported as LSA material. The photo below shows 55-gallon drums containing radioactive waste. Notice that the drums are marked "Radioactive-LSA."

Special Form Radioactive Material - radioactive material which is either a single solid piece or a sealed capsule that can be opened only by destroying the capsule. During accident conditions, special form radioactive material would be non-dispersible and would therefore not present a contamination hazard. Though not a contamination hazard, special form sources may pose a significant radiation hazard. A sealed radioactive source used in radiography operations (like the one pictured below) is an example of a special form radioactive material.

SCO - an acronym that stands for Surface Contaminated Objects. SCO means a solid object that is not in and of itself radioactive, but has radioactive material deposited on any of its surfaces (i.e., contamination). Examples of SCO material would include equipment (pumps, drills, etc.) used in decommissioning activities or contaminated protective clothing.

Transport Index (TI) - The transport index is a single number, determined by the shipper, that is used to provide control over radiation exposure and establish transport controls. The TI appears on Radioactive Yellow II and III labels (see example below) and on the shipping papers. The Transport Index is determined by taking the maximum radiation level (as measured in mrem/hr) at one meter (3.3 feet) from an undamaged package. The transport index can be used by the responder as a good starting point for determining whether damage has occurred to a package. The carrier uses the TI to control the total number of packages allowed on a conveyance. Under normal transport conditions, the sum of all TIs in the transport vehicle can not exceed 50.

COMMON RADIOACTIVE MATERIAL PROPER SHIPPING NAMES

Title 49 of the Code of Federal Regulations (CFR) is where the regulatory requirements for the transport of radioactive materials are found. Title 49 contains the Hazardous Materials Table (HMT), which categorizes material the DOT has designated as hazardous material for purposes of transportation. For each material listed, the HMT provides information on the hazard class, the United Nations Identification Number (UN ID), gives the Proper Shipping Name (PSN), and other information for preparing hazardous material shipments. The PSNs for radioactive material are listed in the table on the following page. These PSNs are also found in the blue pages of the ERG. Note that the words "radioactive material" appear as a part of the PSN for all material listed in the table. Many of the definitions listed on page 6 through 8 of this module appear as part of the PSN.

M E R R T T
Radiological Terminology and Units

Proper Shipping Names	UN ID Number
Radioactive material, excepted package-articles manufactured from natural uranium *or* depleted uranium *or* natural thorium.	UN2909
Radioactive material, excepted package-empty packaging.	UN2908
Radioactive material, excepted package-instruments *or* articles.	UN2911
Radioactive material, excepted package-limited quantity of material.	UN2910
Radioactive material, low specific activity (LSA-I) *non fissile or fissile-excepted.*	UN2912
Radioactive material, low specific activity (LSA-II) *non fissile or fissile-excepted.*	UN3321
Radioactive material, low specific activity (LSA-III) *non fissile or fissile-excepted.*	UN3322
Radioactive material, surface contaminated objects (SCO-I *or* SCO-II) *non fissile or fissile-excepted.*	UN2913
Radioactive material, transported under special arrangement, *non fissile or fissile-excepted.*	UN2919
Radioactive material, transported under special arrangement, fissile.	UN3331
Radioactive material, Type A package, fissile *non-special form.*	UN3327
Radioactive material, Type A package *non-special form, non fissile or fissile-excepted.*	UN2915
Radioactive material, Type A package, special form *non fissile or fissile-excepted.*	UN3332
Radioactive material, Type A package, special form, fissile.	UN3333
Radioactive material, Type B(M) package, fissile.	UN3329
Radioactive material, Type B(M) package *non fissile or fissile-excepted.*	UN2917
Radioactive material, Type B(U) package, fissile.	UN3328
Radioactive material, Type B(U) package *non fissile or fissile-excepted.*	UN2916
Radioactive material, uranium hexafluoride *non fissile or fissile-excepted.*	UN2978
Radioactive material, uranium hexafluoride, fissile.	UN2977

notes

RADIOLOGICAL UNITS

In 1975, the 15th General Conference of Weights and Measures adopted new names for certain basic units in radiation protection technology. These new units are consistent with the metric system or with the International System of Units (SI system) developed by the International Committee for Weights and Measures.

Measuring Radiation

The Roentgen (R) and Rem (Roentgen Equivalent Man)

Radiation exposure is measured in units of roentgen and rem. For our purposes, one roentgen is equal to one rem. Because one roentgen or one rem of radiation is a fairly large amount of radiation, the prefix milli is often used. Milli means one one-thousandth (1/1,000). In other words, there are 1,000 milliroentgens (mR) in one roentgen, or 1,000 millirem (mrem) in one rem. A typical radiation dose from a medical x-ray is about 40 mrem.

According to the National Council on Radiation Protection and Measurements (NCRP), the average person in the United States is exposed to a dose of approximately 360 mrem per year from both man-made and natural sources (NCRP Report No. 93).

In this section, we focus on the traditional units for radiation measurement because they are still widely used in the response community. The SI unit for radiation exposure is the sievert. One sievert is equal to 100 rem.

Measuring Radioactivity

Radioactivity is measured in the number of nuclear transformations or disintegrations that occur in a sample during a specific time. This is known as the activity of the sample. Activity is required (by federal law) to be listed on radiation-warning labels and shipping papers in the SI units. The example above shows a warning label listing the activity of the material inside the package.

The SI unit for activity is the becquerel (Bq), which equals 1 disintegration per second (dps). The conventional unit of activity is the curie (Ci), which is 3.7 x 1010 or 37 billion (37,000,000,000) disintegrations per second. Both the curie and becquerel measure the same thing—activity. Although not required, the activity in curies is sometimes shown on warning labels and/or shipping papers in parentheses after the activity in becquerels. For example, in the illustration on the previous page, the activity listed on the label of 7.4 MBq is equal to 200 µCi. The "M" and "µ" shown before the Becquerel and Curie abbreviations are prefixes. One curie is considered to be a large amount of activity, whereas one becquerel is a very small amount of activity. To account for this, prefixes are often used to change the size of the unit. Many of the commonly used prefixes are shown in the table below.

Symbol	Prefix	Prefix Value	Example
p	pico	1 trillionth, or 10^{-12}	pCi = one trillionth of a curie
n	nano	1 billionth, or 10^{-9}	nCi = one billionth of a curie
µ	micro	1 millionth, or 10^{-6}	µCi = one millionth of a curie
m	milli	1 thousandth, or 10^{-3}	mCi = one thousandth of a curie
k	kilo	1 thousand, or 10^{3}	kBq = one thousand becquerel
M	Mega	1 million, or 10^{6}	MBq = one million becquerel
G	Giga	1 billion, or 10^{9}	GBq = one billion becquerel
T	Tera	1 trillion, or 10^{12}	TBq = one trillion becquerel
P	Peta	1 quadrillion, or 10^{15}	PBq = one quadrillion becquerel

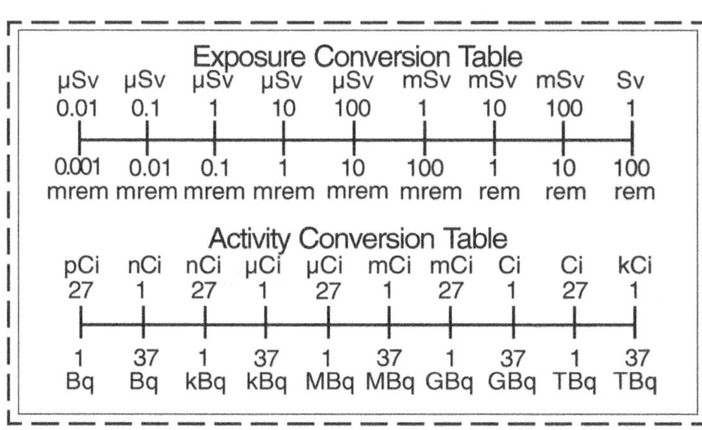

notes

Activity may also be expressed as a measure of its concentration or specific activity. Common terms for measuring specific activity are Ci/g (curies per gram) and Bq/kg (becquerels per kilogram). It is important to note that there is no direct relationship between activity and the physical quantity of material present. Very high activity material can come in very small packages. For example, one gram of cobalt-60 (commonly used in radiation therapy) has an activity of about 42 TBq or 42 trillion disintegrations per second. On the other hand, one gram of thorium-232 (the radioactive material found in some lantern mantles) has an activity of about 4 kBq or 4,000 disintegrations per second. Therefore, you would need to have well over 10 billion grams (23,000 pounds) of thorium-232 to equal the activity in one gram of cobalt-60.

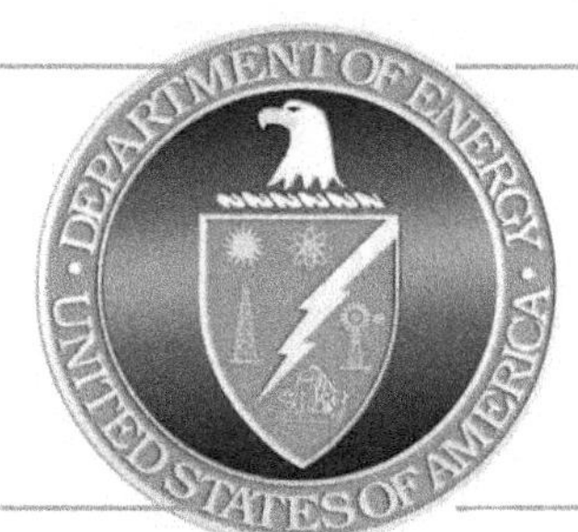

Check Your Understanding

1. The four basic types of ionizing radiation are ______, ____, ______and ________.

2. ______ ________ is defined by DOT regulations as plutonium-239, plutonium-241, uranium-233, uranium-235, or any combination of these radionuclides.

3. ________ form radioactive material is radioactive material which is either a single solid piece or a sealed capsule that can be opened only by destroying the capsule.

4. The _________ ______ is assigned to a package by taking the maximum radiation level (as measured in mrem/hr) at one meter (3.3 feet) from an undamaged package.

5. The ________ and ____ are two units used to measure radiation exposure.

6. The SI unit for measuring radioactivity (activity) is the ________.

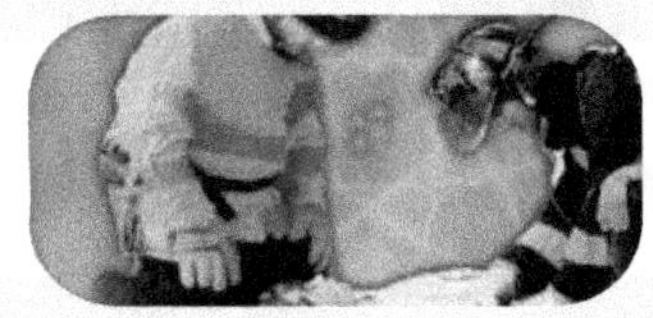

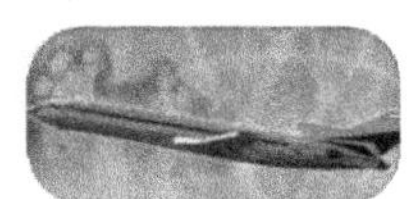
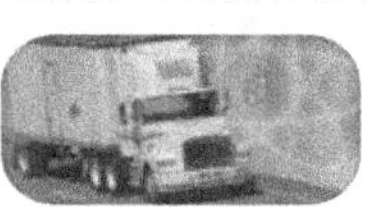

ANSWERS

1. alpha
   beta
   gamma
   neutron
2. Fissile material
3. Special
4. transport index
5. roentgen
   rem
6. becquerel

notes

INTRODUCTION

This module provides general information about radiological survey instruments. Basic functions and limitations are discussed. Because there are many models of survey instruments available, this discussion provides only a general description of survey instrument types and uses. For participants wanting more detailed descriptions of specific devices and their functions, information on several commonly available instruments is included in the appendix to this module.

PURPOSE

The purpose of this module is to provide you with a general awareness and understanding of radiological survey instruments and how they can be used to survey for radiation exposure and contamination. Proper use of radiological survey instruments will provide you with more information on the hazards present at the scene.

MODULE OBJECTIVES

Upon completion of this module, you will be able to:

1. Identify two categories of radiological survey instruments.
2. State the proper application and limitation of contamination survey instruments.
3. State the proper application and limitation of radiation exposure survey instruments.
4. Identify commonly used dosimetry devices.

notes

RADIOLOGICAL SURVEYS AND INSTRUMENTATION

The use of radiological survey instrumentation by responders at an incident scene is optional. The Emergency Response Guidebook does not specifically recommend the use of radiological survey instruments during the initial response phase of the incident. Use of these instruments will give you more detailed information about the radiological hazards present at the scene.

Radiation cannot be detected by our senses. By using radiological survey instruments, properly trained responders can easily and accurately detect radiation. There are two general categories of radiological survey instruments available. One category of instruments is designed to measure radiation, while the other is designed to measure contamination. Some instruments are designed to measure both radiation and contamination.

Basic Theory

Similar to the way a radio converts radio waves to sound, a radiological survey instrument converts radiation energy to a meter reading. In a radiological survey instrument, ionizing radiation interacts with material in the detector to produce ions. The detector collects these ions and sends them to the instrument which produces an audible and/or visual response. Some radiological survey instruments combine the detector and meter in one unit, while others may have the detector attached to the meter by a cable (*See examples below*).

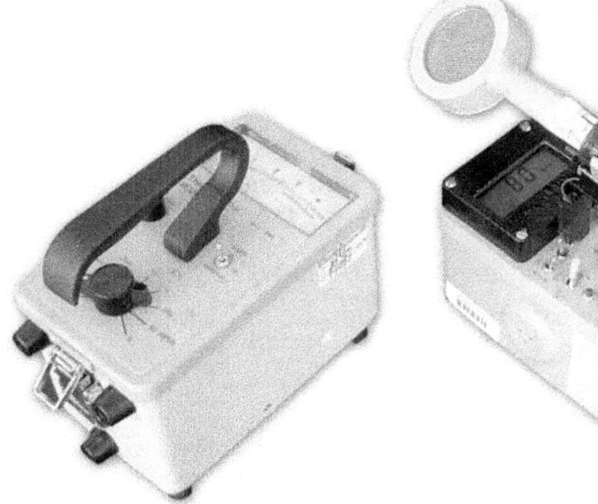

M E R R T T
Radiological Survey Instruments and Dosimetry Devices

There are many different models and types of radiological survey instruments with a variety of features and controls[1]. Because they have different operating characteristics, you should know how to operate those used in your jurisdiction.

Contamination Survey Instruments

Contamination survey instruments are very sensitive and measure the presence of radioactive material in terms of counts per minute (CPM). Instruments that measure effects in CPM are useful for detecting contamination on personnel and equipment. A limitation of contamination survey instruments is that they should not be used to measure radiation exposure. Contamination surveys should always be reported in CPM.

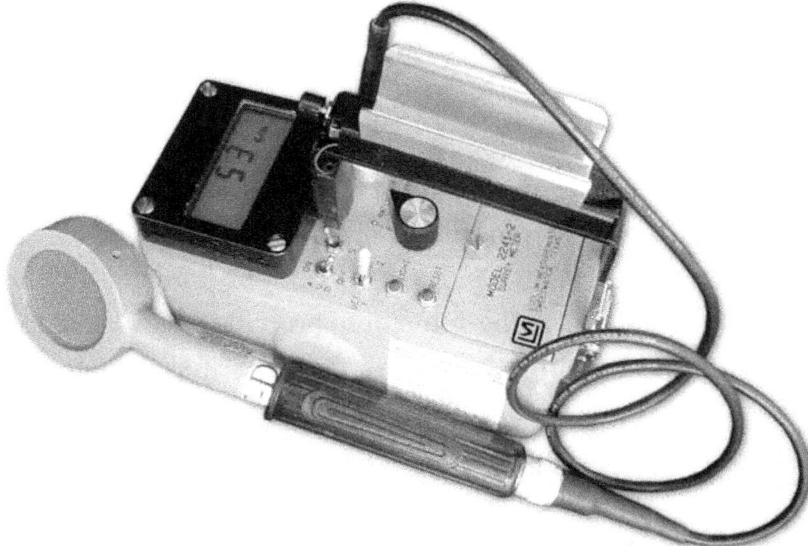

Application of Contamination Survey Instruments

The purpose of a contamination survey is to locate radioactive material in unwanted locations. Contamination surveys are useful for the following:

- Locating contamination on personnel and equipment
- Determining the effectiveness of decontamination
- Verifying contamination control boundaries
- Determining the extent and magnitude of a contaminated area

---

[1] Descriptions of some of the instruments commonly used by responders, including the CD V-700 and the CD V-715 Survey Meters, can be found in the appendix to this module.

notes

Because the difference between measurements of background radiation and that produced by contamination may be slight, it is important to determine the background (naturally-occurring) radiation level prior to performing a survey. Determine background radiation levels by observing the meter reading in the cold zone. Contamination surveys should be preformed in areas with low background radiation. The higher the background radiation level, the harder it is to determine contamination levels.

Begin by following your local procedures or manufacturer's recommendations for instrument pre-operational checks and instrument calibration frequency.

- Verify that the instrument is on, set to the lowest scale, the audio can be heard, and there is visual response
- The probe/detector should be held within 1/2 inch of the surface being surveyed
- Move the probe slowly, approximately 1 to 2 inches per second
- If the count rate increases while surveying, pause for 5-10 seconds over the area to provide adequate time for instrument response

Become familiar with your jurisdiction's or state's guidelines for when an individual or object is considered contaminated. For example, some jurisdictions use twice background or 100 CPM above background as a positive indication of contamination.

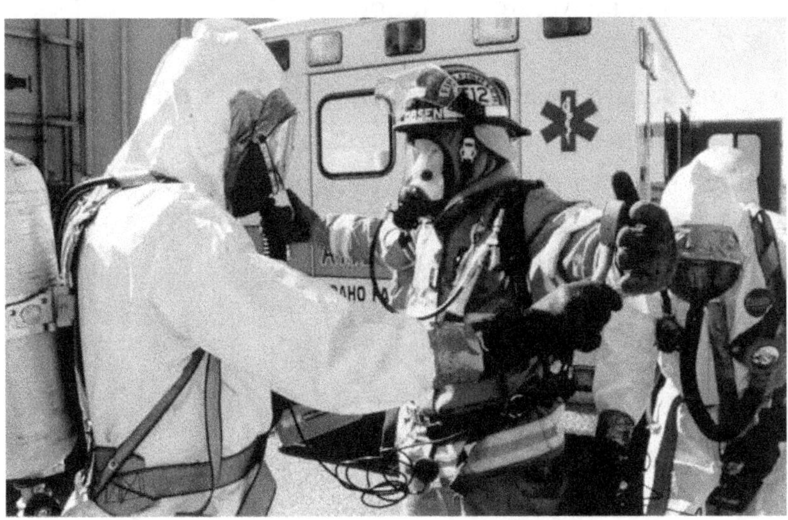

Radiation Exposure Survey Instruments

Exposure rate survey instruments usually measure radiation in terms of milliroentgen per hour (mR/hr) or roentgen per hour (R/hr). These effects are typically recorded in the biological equivalent of mrem/hour or rem/hour or, if the instrument uses the SI units, micro or milli sieverts/hour. Instruments that measure effects in mR/hr or R/hr are most useful for measuring radiation fields at the event scene. A limitation of radiation exposure survey instruments is that they are generally not as sensitive as contamination survey instruments and may not efficiently detect some types of contamination.

Application of Radiation Exposure Survey Instruments

The purpose of a radiation exposure survey is to locate and measure sources of radiation. Radiation exposure surveys are useful for the following:

- Establishing control zone boundaries
- Controlling personnel exposure
- Assessing package integrity
- Locating sources of radiation

Follow your local procedures or manufacturer's recommendations on instrument pre-operational checks and instrument calibration frequency. Prior to performing a radiation survey, verify that the instrument is on, the range selector switch is on the lowest scale, the audio can be heard (if applicable), and a visual response registers on the meter.

notes

Many radiation exposure rate survey instruments are designed to detect both beta and gamma radiation. These instruments typically employ some type of rotating or movable beta shield that can be opened to admit beta radiation (see photos below). With the detector shield closed, beta radiation is blocked out and only gamma radiation is detected. With the beta shield open, both beta and gamma radiation are detected. The beta dose contribution from a measurement can be determined by subtracting the reading taken with the beta shield closed from the reading taken with the beta shield open (open window reading – closed window reading).

When surveying for beta and gamma radiation, radiation measurements should be made by approaching the area or object to be surveyed with the detector extended in front of you and the beta shield, if applicable, in the open position. With the shield in the open position, the instrument will simultaneously detect gamma and beta radiation.

Periodically monitor in a 360 degree circle to ensure that you have not walked by a source of radiation. Monitor for radiation with the detector at waist level and periodically check above and below this level. When a source of radiation is discovered, survey as necessary to determine its approximate location.

When performing a radiation survey, it is useful to listen to the audio response so that even if you are temporarily distracted, the response to a radiation field can be heard.

The following table can be used to assist you in converting the SI units (sieverts) to the traditional units (millirem).

Reading in sieverts	Equals	Reading in mrem & rem
1 microsievert	=	0.1 millirem
1 millisievert	=	100 millirem
1 sievert	=	100 rem

READING THE METER FACE

Many of the newer survey instruments have a digital display and will automatically adjust the range from microrem to millirem to rem per hour or from counts per minute (CPM) to kilo counts per minute (kCPM). The traditional analog instruments can be more difficult to read than digital instruments. Often it requires that the user multiply the reading displayed on the meter face by a multiplier, depending on which scale the instrument range multiplier switch is set to. For example, in the illustration below, the reading on the meter face shows a reading of 200 CPM; since the range multiplier switch is set to X10, the 200 is multiplied by 10 so that the actual reading is 2,000 CPM.

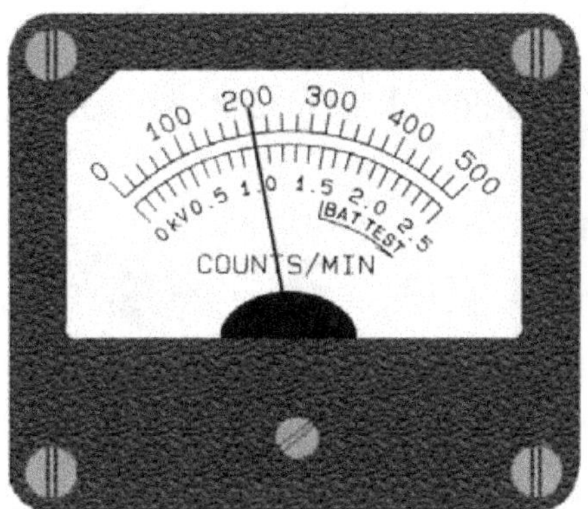

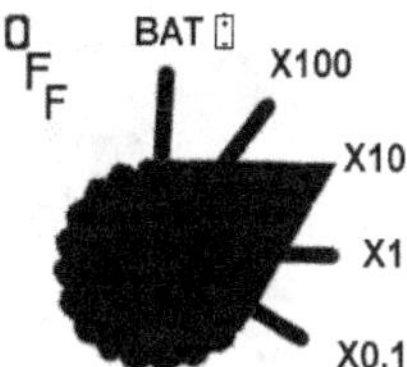

As discussed earlier, contamination survey results are usually recorded in CPM and radiation survey results are usually recorded in mR/hr. For those instruments that display in both CPM and mR/hr, the user should determine which units to record their reading in based upon the type of survey (radiation or contamination) being performed. Contamination surveys are best performed with pancake style detectors and radiation surveys are best performed with side window GM or "hotdog" style detectors. An example of each type is shown below:

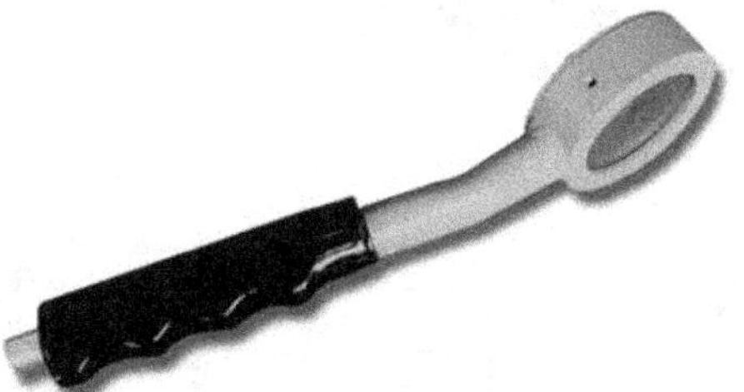

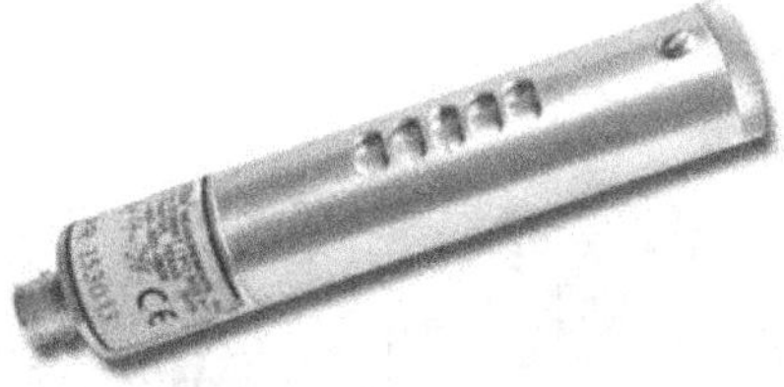

Pancake Style Probe   **Hotdog Style Probe**

In the case of the CD V-700 (pictured at right), the meter face reads in both CPM and mR/hr. When using this type of survey instrument with the standard side window GM or "hotdog" probe (as seen in the photo to the right), readings should be recorded in mR/hr when the probe window is closed and in CPM when the probe window is open.

With the Ludlum style instruments, readings should be recorded in CPM with the pancake style probe attached and in mR/hr with the hotdog probe attached. The graphics below illustrate these points.

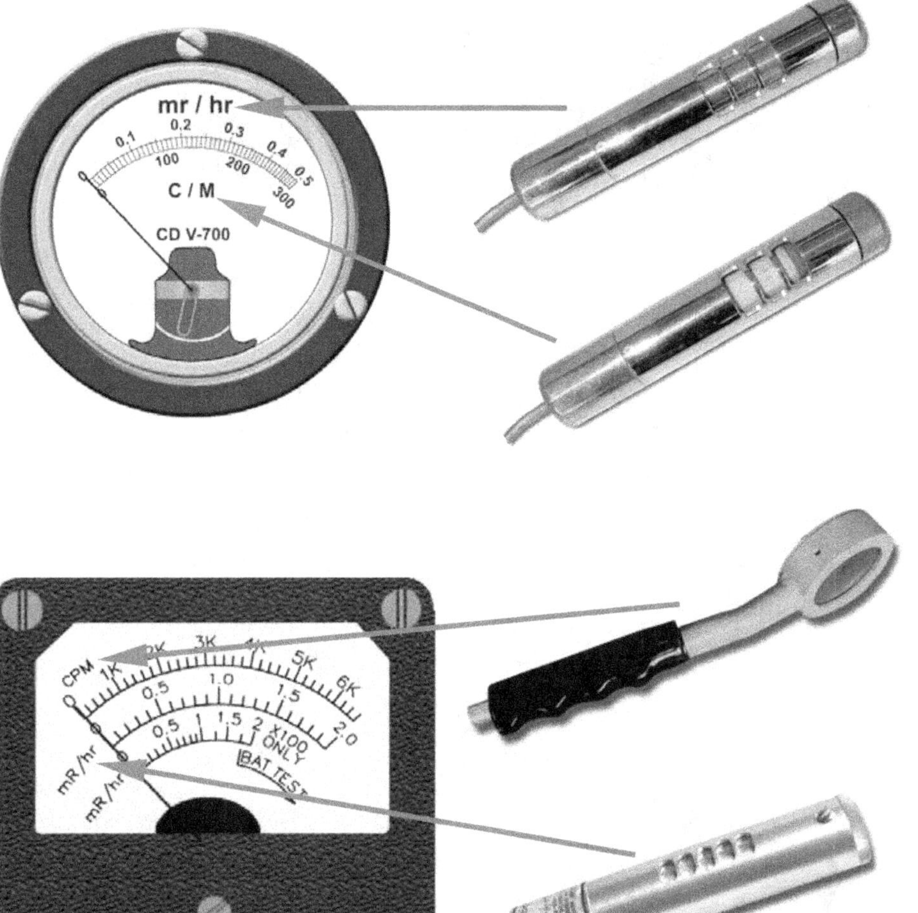

notes

DOSIMETRY DEVICES

Although not required at an incident scene, dosimetry devices are useful for keeping track of your total accumulated radiation dose. A dosimeter is like the odometer on your car. For example, where the odometer measures total miles traveled, the dosimeter measures the total amount of dose you have received. There are several different types of dosimeters available. Some commonly used examples are discussed here.

Self Reading Dosimeters

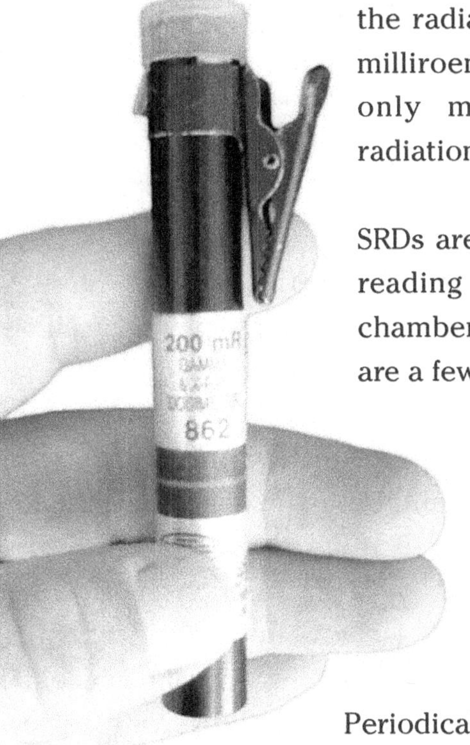

A self reading dosimeter (SRD) measures the radiation dose in roentgens (R) or milliroentgens (mR). Generally, SRDs only measure gamma and X-ray radiation.

SRDs are called by many names: direct reading dosimeter (DRD), pocket ion chamber (PIC), and pencil dosimeters are a few common names.

To read the dosimeter, hold it up to a light source and look through the eyepiece. You should always record the SRD reading before you enter a radiation field (hot zone). Periodically, (at 15 to 30 minute intervals) read your SRD while working in the hot zone and upon exit from the hot zone. If a higher-than-expected reading is indicated, or if the SRD reading is off-scale, you should:

- Notify others in the hot zone
- Have them check their SRDs
- Exit the hot zone immediately
- Follow local reporting procedures

If you are using a low range dosimeter (e.g., 0 to 200 mR), you should consider exiting the hot zone if the dosimeter reads greater than 75% of full scale. The reason for this is to prevent your dosimeter from going off scale; if your dosimeter goes off scale, it will no longer keep a record of the dose you received. A dosimeter can be recharged or "zeroed" after each use. Record the final reading upon leaving the hot zone. Exercise care when using a SRD, they are sensitive instruments. Rough handling, static electricity, or dropping a dosimeter may result in erroneous or off-scale readings.

Electronic Dosimeters

The electronic dosimeter serves the same basic function as the SRD, except that it has a digital readout that displays the total dose received by the wearer in milliroentgens (mR) or millirem (mrem).

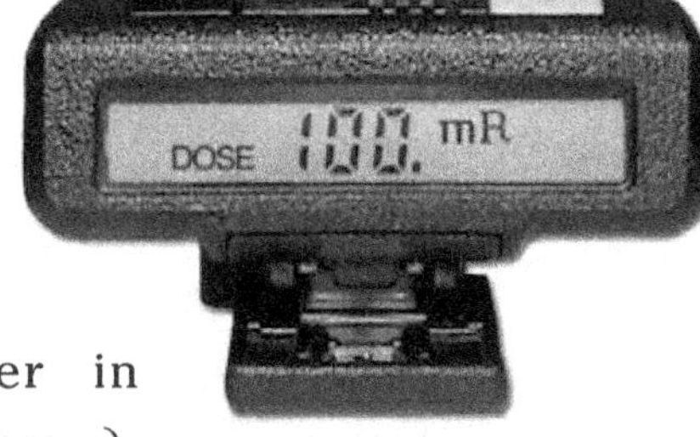

Electronic dosimeters are available from various manufacturers in a variety of sizes and shapes. There are many options available, depending on the required or desired response.

Many electronic dosimeters have an audible response that indicates the exposure rate through a series of chirping noises. The frequency of the chirping increases and decreases in relation to the dose rate. These "chirpers" provide the advantage of an audible warning when dose rates increase.

notes

Thermoluminescent Dosimeters

Thermoluminescent dosimeters (TLDs) do not provide an "on-the-spot" indication of accumulated dose as the previously mentioned dosimeters do. Specialized equipment is needed to retrieve the radiological exposure data stored by the TLD. TLDs are not usually available for use by individual fire departments or local agencies. Specialized hazardous material response teams and state and federal radiological response organizations usually wear TLDs.

Check Your *Understanding*

1. Radiation itself (can/cannot) be detected by our senses (circle the correct answer).

2. Radiation (can/cannot) be measured easily and accurately (circle the correct answer).

3. Some radiological survey instruments are used to survey for __________, and others are used to detect and/or measure __________ exposure.

4. If a radiological survey instrument measures effects in counts per minute (CPM), it is going to be most useful as a contamination survey instrument. True/False.

5. A limitation of contamination survey instruments is that they are not designed to measure __________ exposure.

6. Exposure rate survey instruments usually measure radiation in terms of __________ per hour or __________ per hour.

7. Some survey Instruments are designed to measure both contamination and radiation exposure. True/False.

8. The purpose of a contamination survey is to locate radioactive material in unwanted locations. True/False.

9. A self reading dosimeter (SRD) keeps track of accumulated (radiation/ contamination) dose while in a field of radiation. (Circle the correct answer).

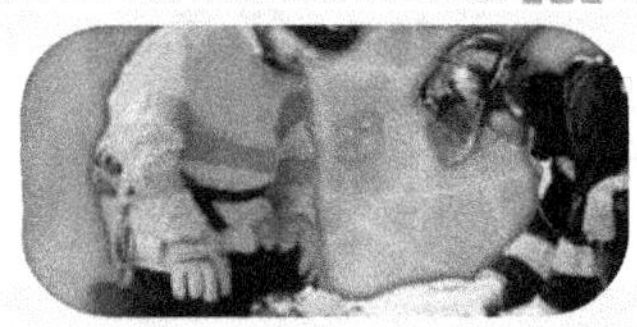
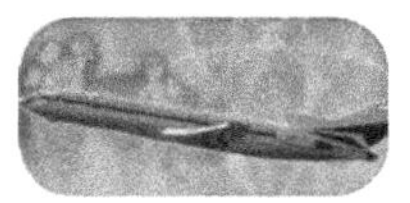

ANSWERS

1. cannot
2. can
3. contamination radiation
4. true
5. radiation
6. milliroentgen roentgen
7. true
8. true
9. radiation

Ludlum Instrument

Meter Reading	**Range Selector**	**Probe Used**	**Results**
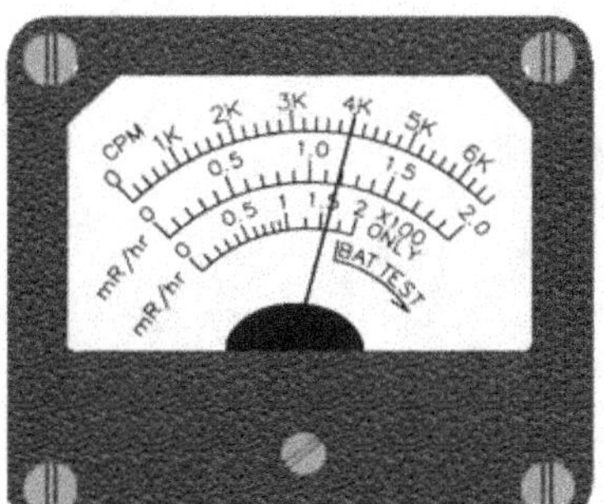	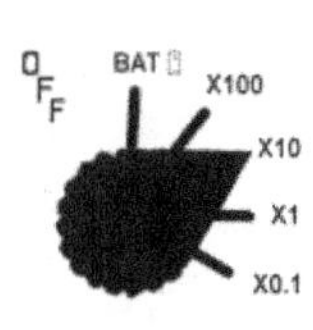	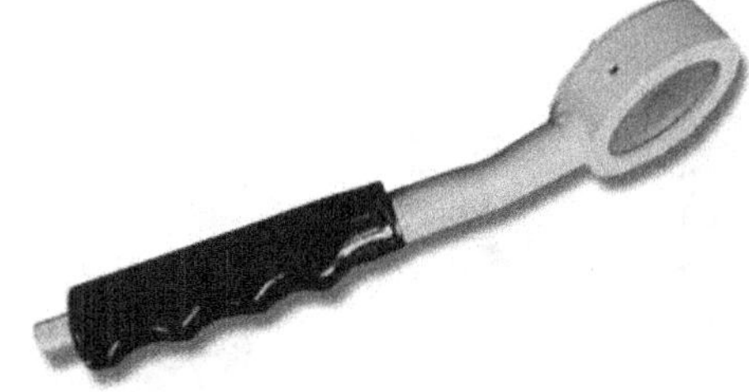	_________
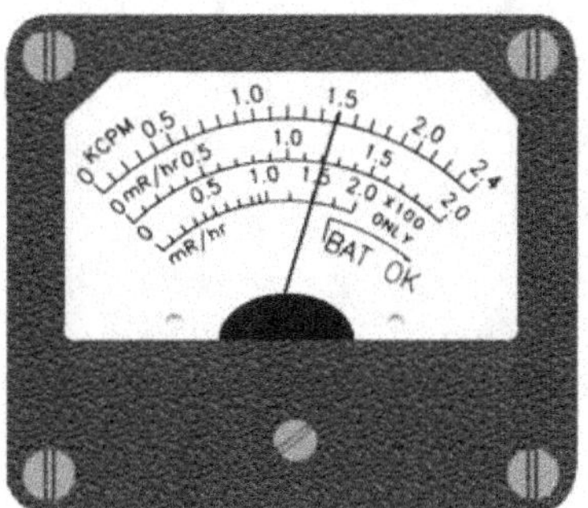	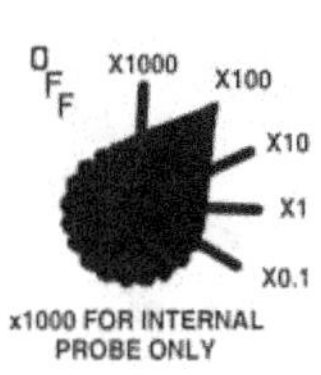	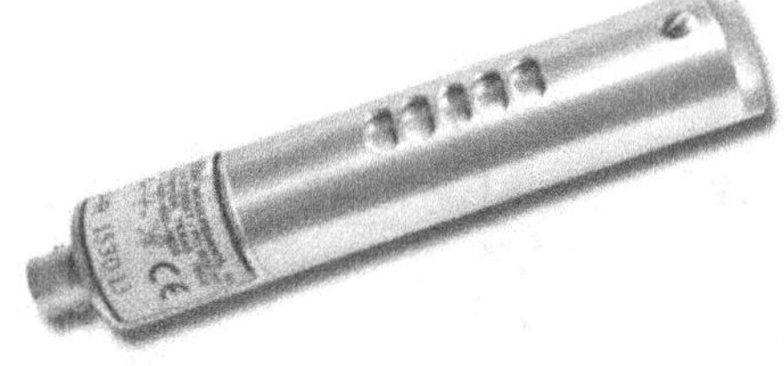	_________
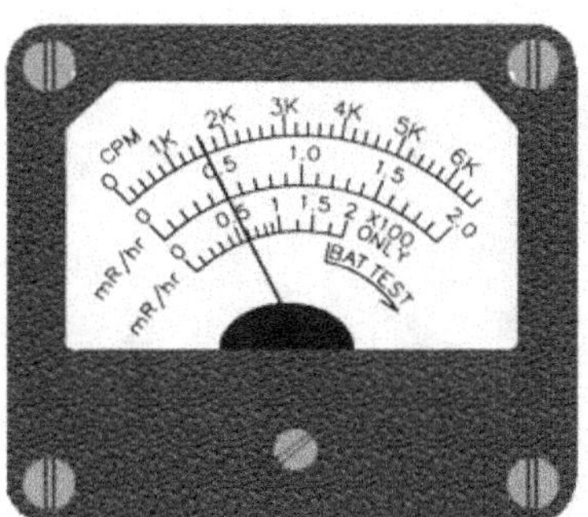	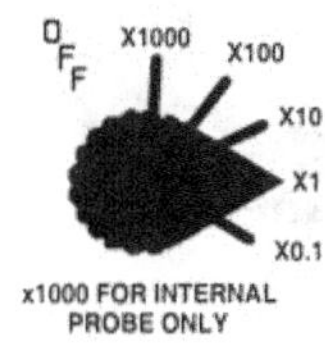	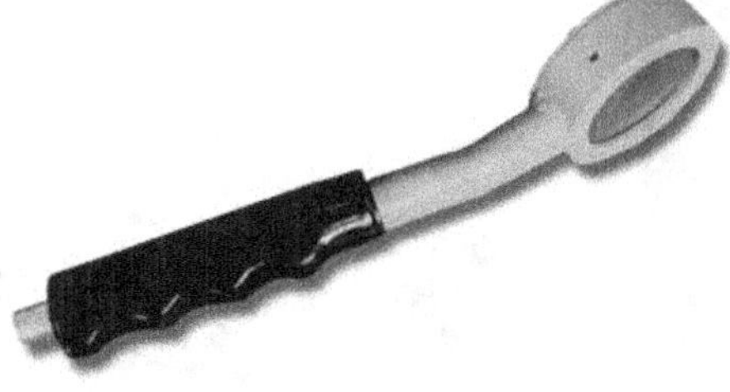	_________
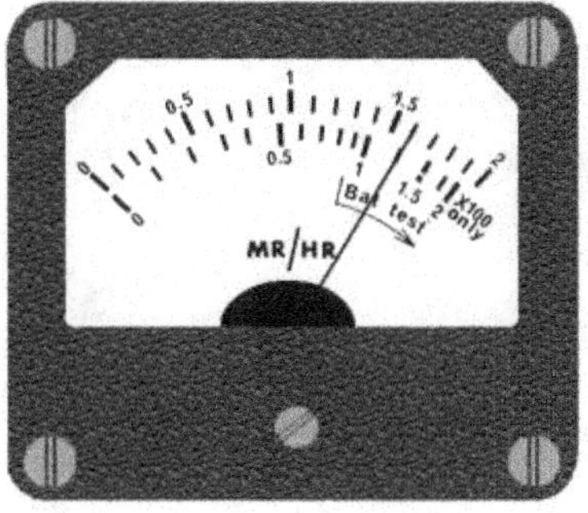	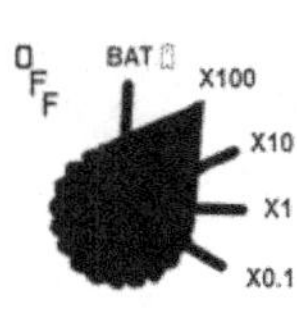	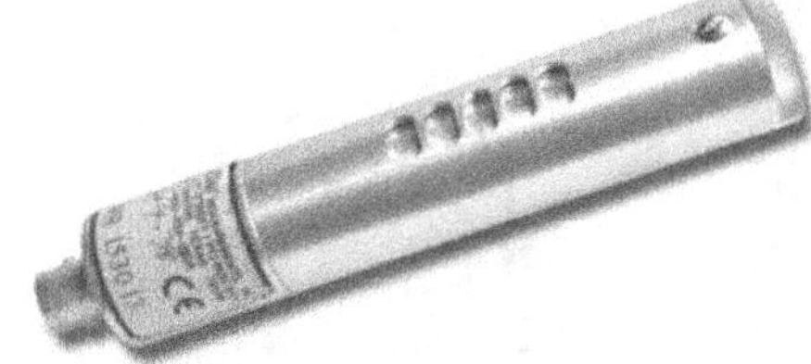	_________

Ludlum Instrument

Meter Reading	Range Selector	Probe Used	Results
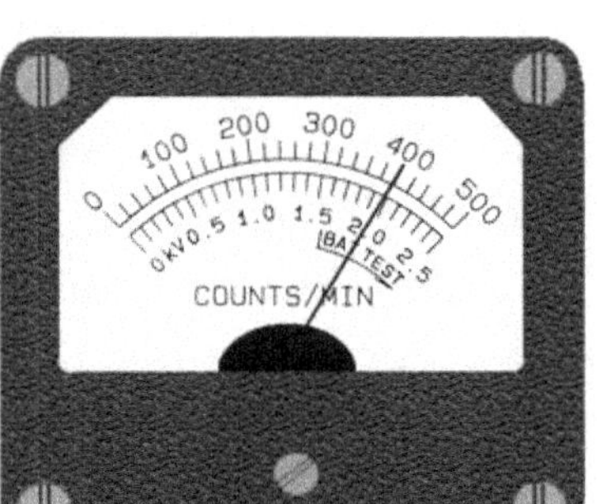		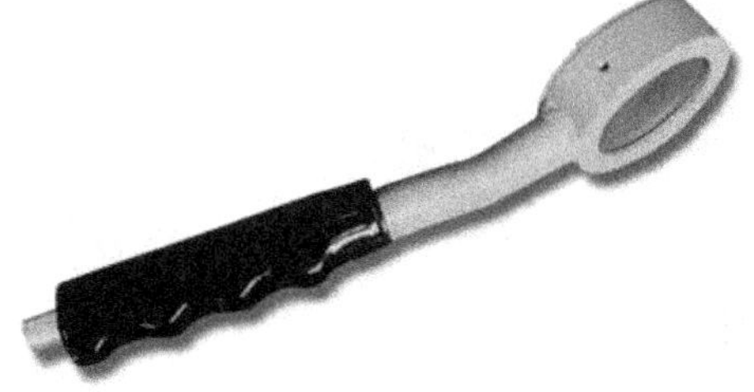	__________
	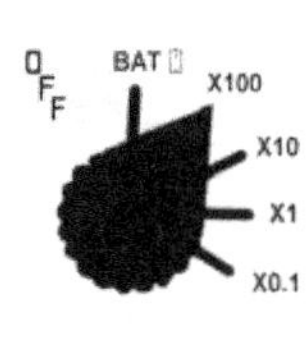	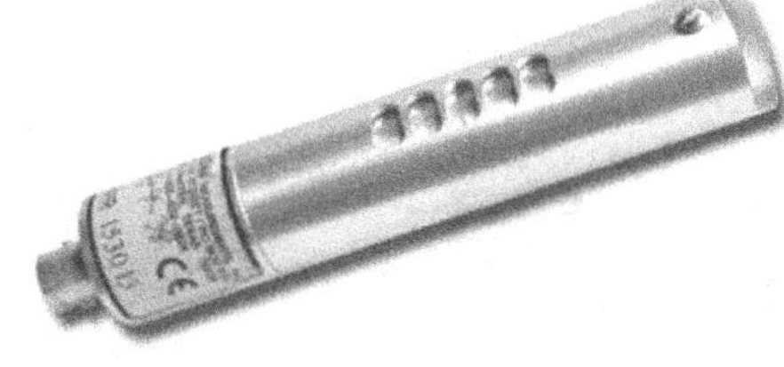	__________
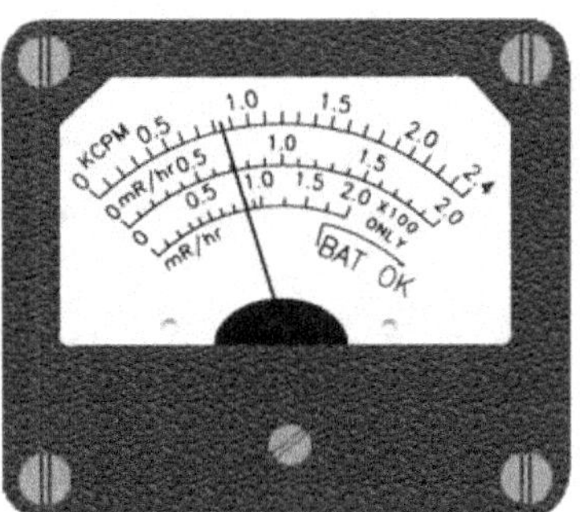	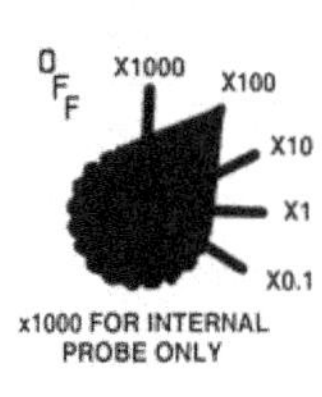	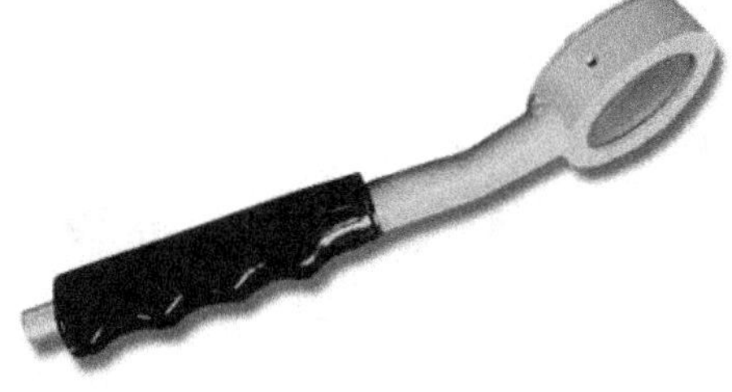	__________
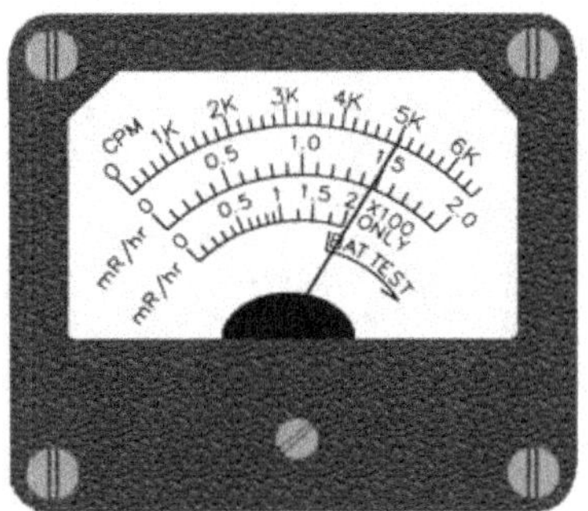	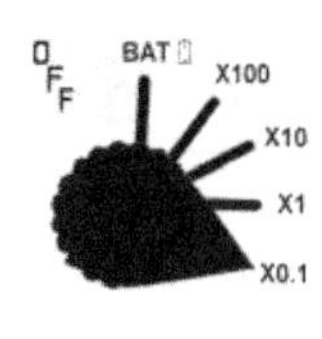	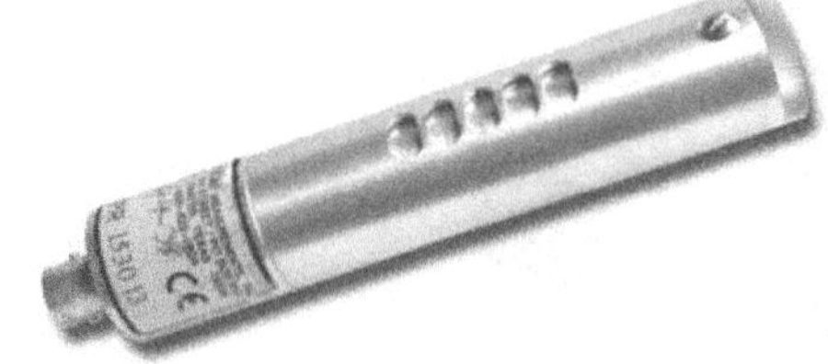	__________

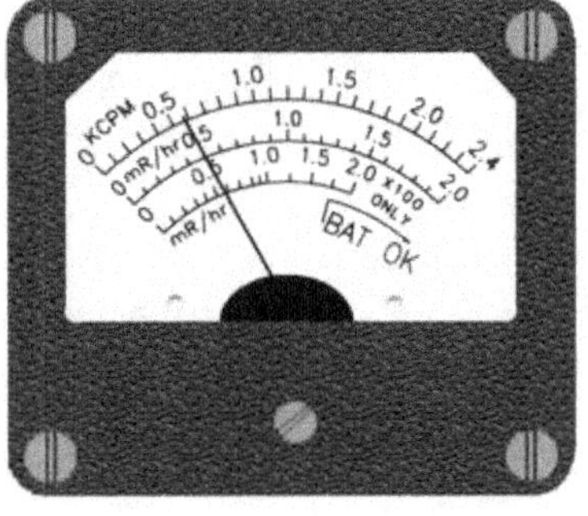
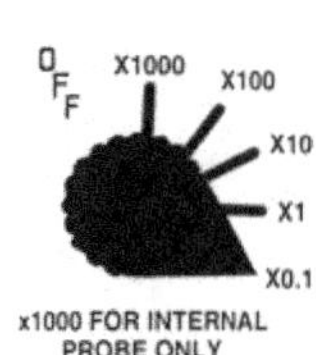

CD V-700 Instrument

Meter Reading	Range Selector	Probe Window	Results

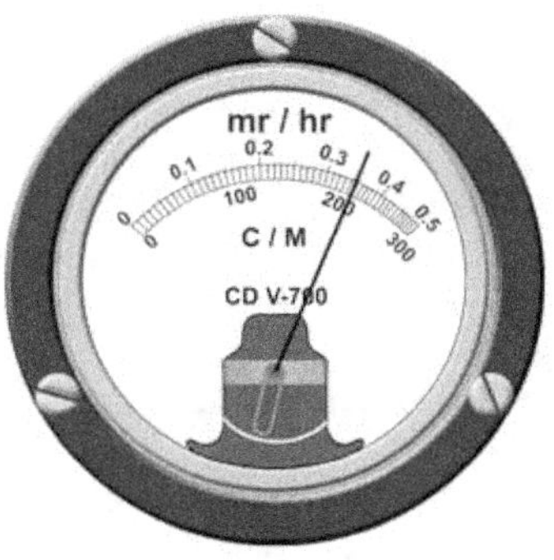 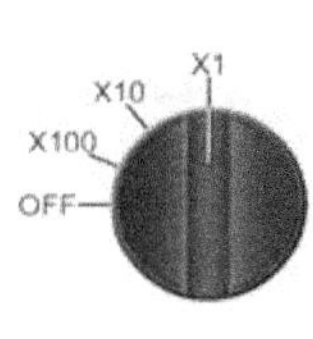 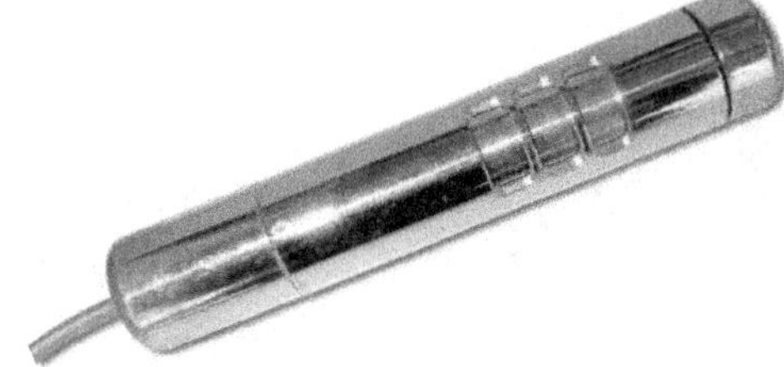

____

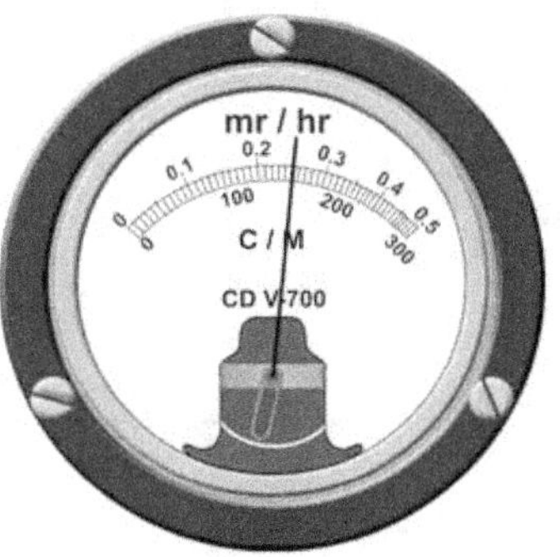 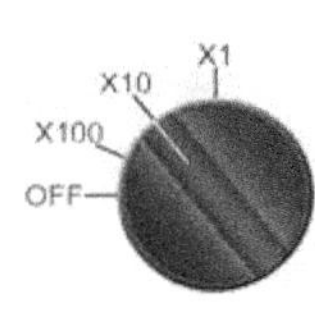 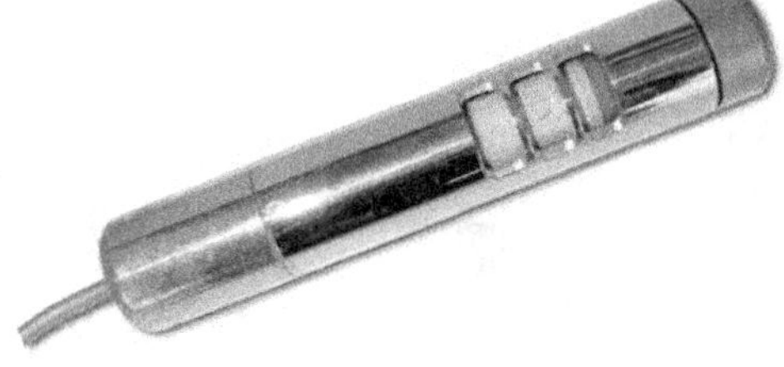

____

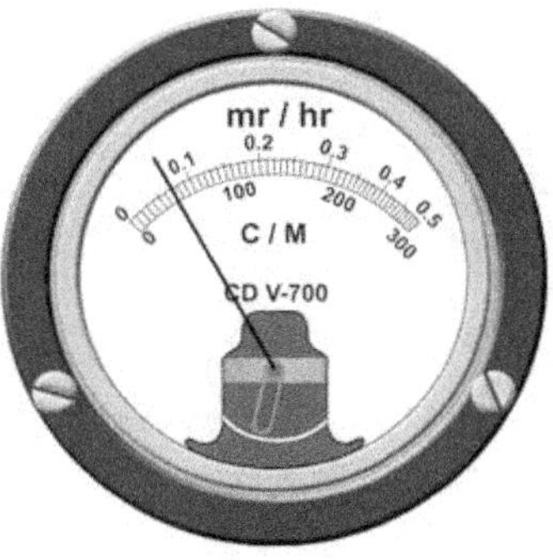 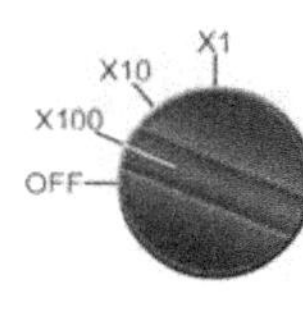 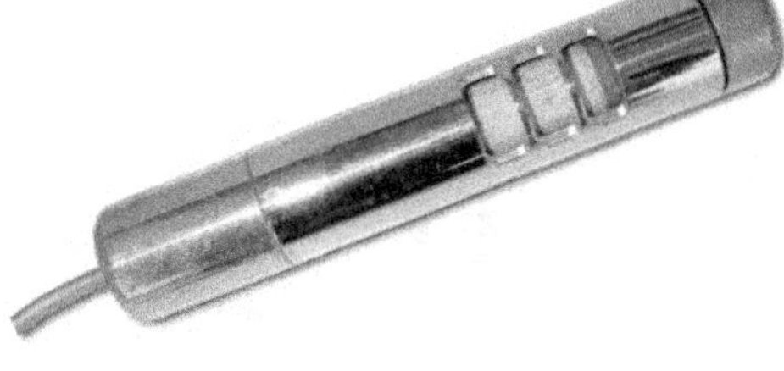

____

 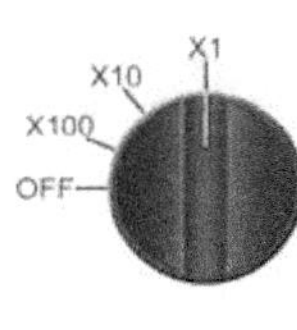 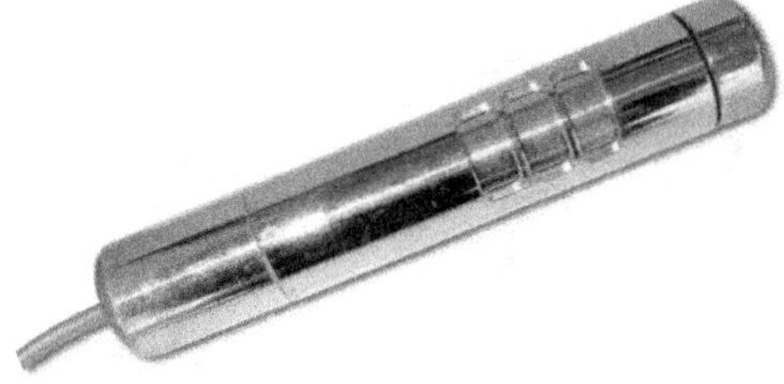

____

CD V-700 Instrument

Meter Reading	Range Selector	Probe Window	Results

 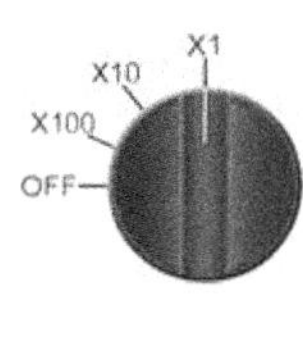 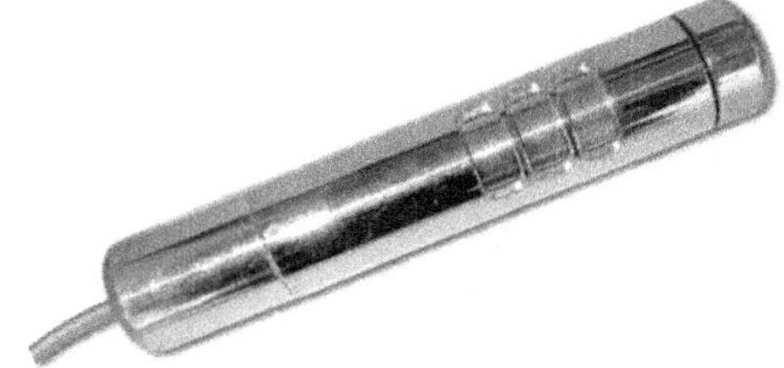

____

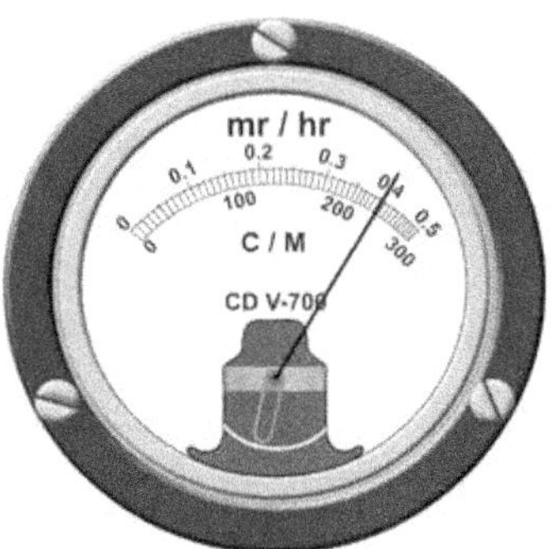 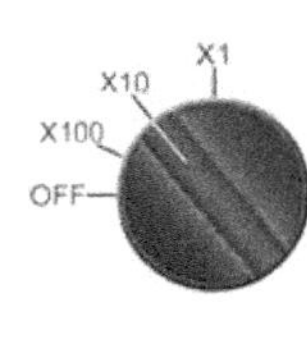 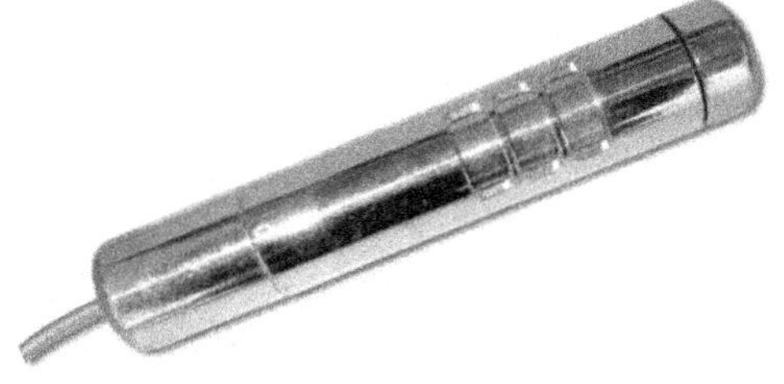

____

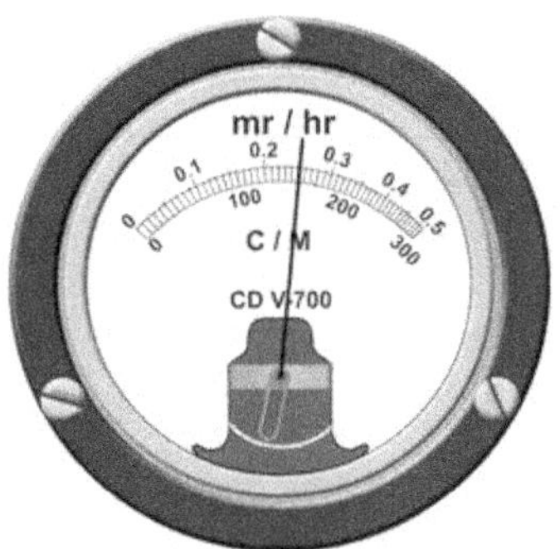 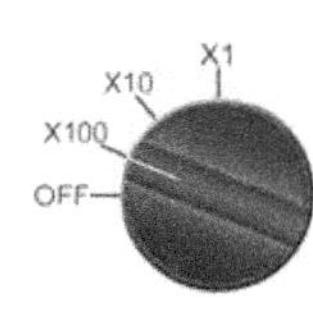 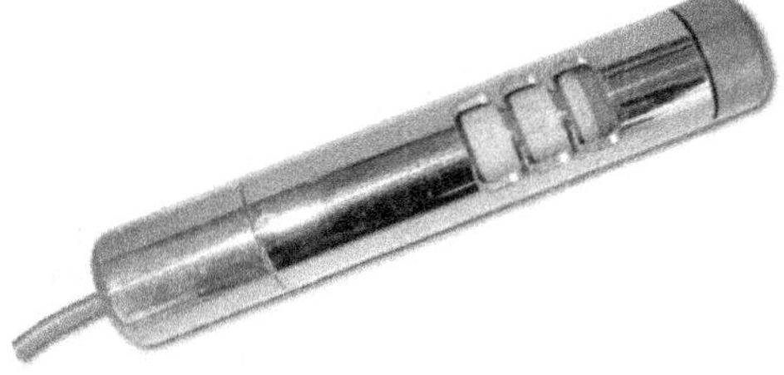

____

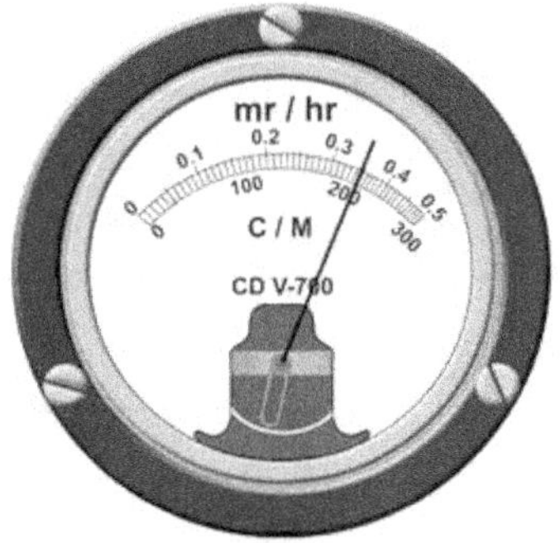 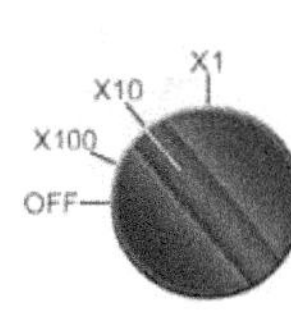 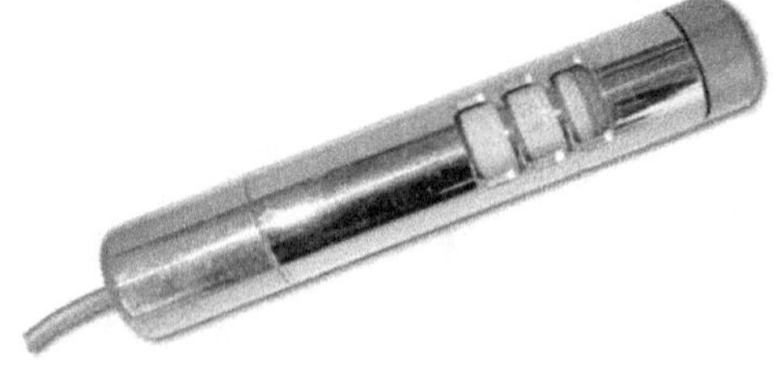

____

M E R R T T
Assessing Package Integrity

INTRODUCTION

The federal government regulates radioactive material packaging, labeling, and transport. The labels used on packages of radioactive material can be used to help you obtain information about the activity and radiation level of the material within the package. Having knowledge of the radiation levels associated with packages of radioactive material can help you determine whether damage to a package has occurred.

This module provides information about radioactive material packaging and radiation levels associated with the radiation-warning labels used in radioactive material transport.

PURPOSE

The purpose of this module is to increase your understanding of the information contained on warning labels and the radiation levels associated with radioactive material packages. Being able to correctly read the warning labels can help you assess the radioactive material package integrity, which in turn will improve your ability to respond safely.

MODULE OBJECTIVES

Upon completion of this module, you will be able to:

1. Identify radiation levels associated with the various radiation-warning labels.
2. Identify the importance of the transport index in determining package integrity.
3. Identify the maximum radiation levels expected on shipping packages and/or transport vehicles.

M E R R T T
Assessing Package Integrity

RADIATION LEVELS ASSOCIATED WITH RADIOACTIVE MATERIAL PACKAGES

The U.S. Government regulates domestic shipments of radioactive material. The U.S. Nuclear Regulatory Commission (NRC) and the U.S. Department of Transportation (DOT) share this responsibility. The areas regulated include the packaging, contents, radiation levels, and various transport requirements, including labeling and shipping papers.

Before transport, shippers of radioactive material are required to check the radiation levels of packages to ensure that all levels are within allowed limits. Radiation levels are checked on the packaging surface and at one meter (3.3 feet) from the package.

TRANSPORT INDEX (TI)

The transport index, often called the TI, is the dimensionless number[1] placed on the label of a package to designate the degree of control to be exercised by the carrier during transportation. The TI is equal to the maximum radiation level in mrem/hour at one meter from an undamaged package. The TI can be an indicator for determining the external radiation hazard of an undamaged package and can be a starting point for determining whether or not damage has occurred.

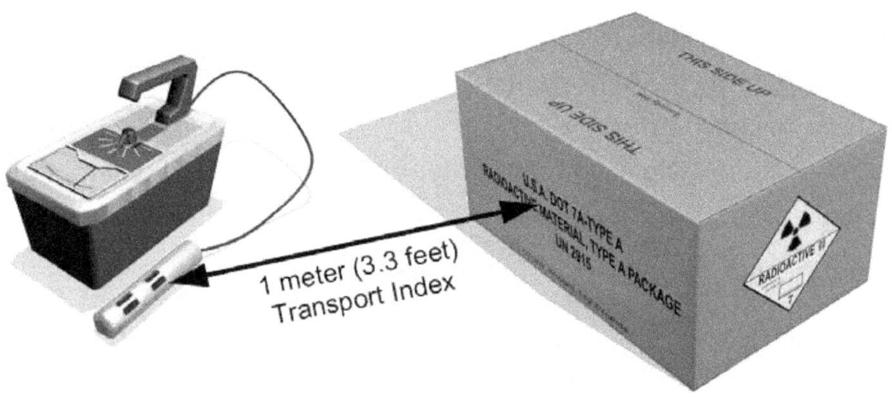

---

[1] Dimensionless number means that there are no units of measure (e.g., mrem) associated with the transport index.

For example, a package with a Radioactive Yellow-III label attached and a TI marked on the label of 2.5 should read between 50 to 200 mrem/hour on contact with the package and 2.5 mrem/hour at one meter from the package. A reading of 5 mrem/hour one meter from this type of package indicates potential damage.

SHIPPING LABELS

After checking radiation levels at a package's surface and at one meter, shippers will attach a radiation-warning label to the package. Radiation-warning labels are attached to opposite sides of each package. Three different labels are applied based on contact and one meter radiation levels: Radioactive White-I, Radioactive Yellow-II, and Radioactive Yellow-III.

Radiation-warning labels will specify the contents and the activity of the material inside the package. In addition, Radioactive Yellow-II and Radioactive Yellow-III labels also specify the TI.

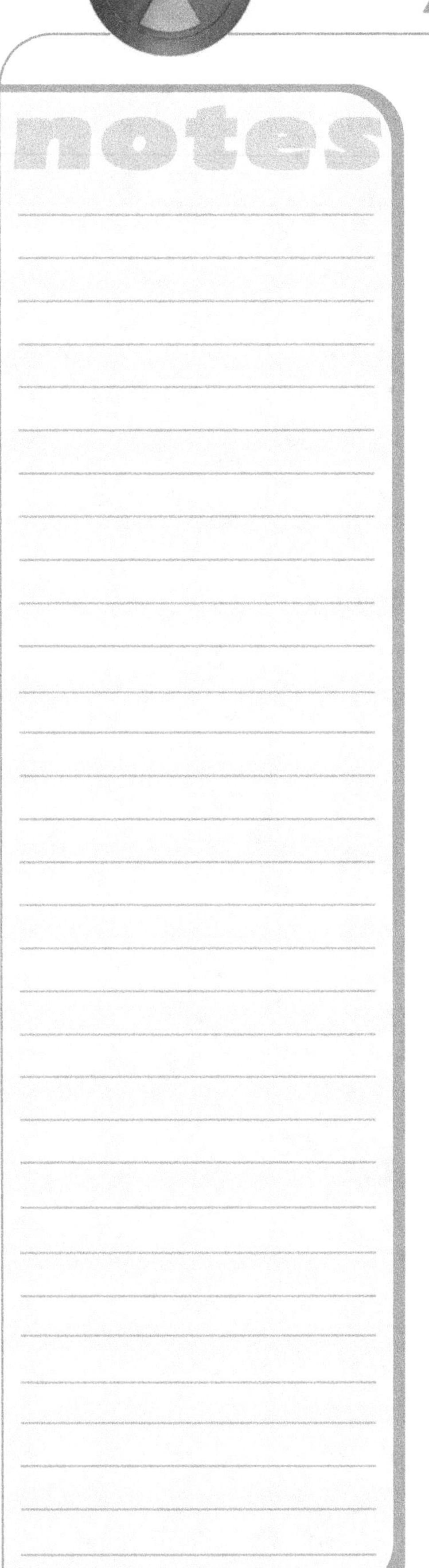

Radioactive White-I

The Radioactive White-I label is attached to packages with extremely low levels of external radiation. The maximum contact radiation level associated with this label is 0.5 mrem/hour.

Radioactive Yellow-II

The Radioactive Yellow-II label is attached to packages with external contact radiation levels ranging from greater than 0.5 mrem/hour to no more than 50 mrem/hour.

The Radioactive Yellow-II label also has a box for the transport index. The maximum allowable transport index for this label is 1.

M E R R T T
Assessing Package Integrity

Radioactive Yellow-III

The Radioactive Yellow-III label is attached to packages with external contact radiation levels ranging from greater than 50 mrem/hour to a maximum of 200 mrem/hour.

The maximum allowable transport index for this label is 10.

Category of Label	Maximum Contact Dose Rate	Maximum Dose Rate at 1 Meter
White-I	0.5 mrem/hr	N/A
Yellow-II	50 mrem/hr	1 mrem/hr
Yellow-III	200 mrem/hr	10 mrem/hr

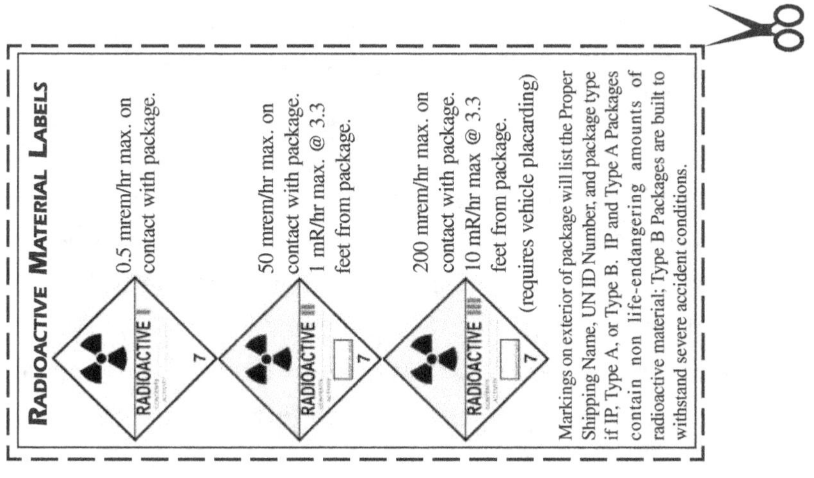

M E R R T T
Assessing Package Integrity

ASSESSING PACKAGE AND VEHICLE RADIATION LIMITS

Radiation Limits on Packages in Non-exclusive Use Shipments

When radioactive material is transported under normal conditions (non-exclusive use), each **package** must be designed and prepared for shipment so that the maximum radiation level does not exceed 200 mrem/hour at

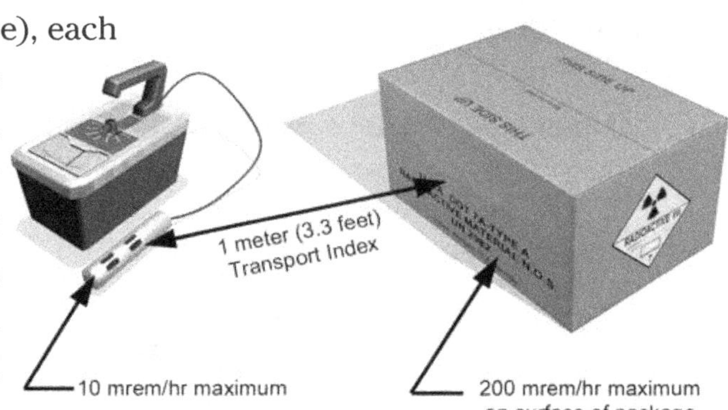

any point on the external surface of the package and the transport index does not exceed 10. When assessing a package's integrity at an accident scene, you can use this information as a baseline for determining if damage has occurred to the package. For example, a dose rate reading of 250 mrem/hour on contact with the exterior of a package could indicate potential damage.

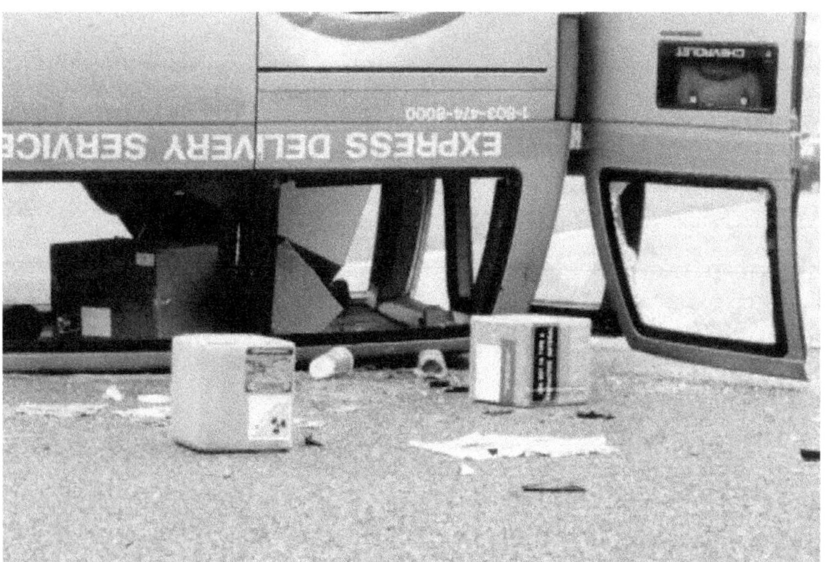

Additionally, you should not expect to see radiation dose rates on the surface of the **vehicle** transporting the material that are greater than the limits allowed for the packages inside the vehicle. An exception might occur if several packages with dose rates close to 200 mrem/hour were located near the exterior surface of a vehicle; in such a case, you may see a dose rate reading on the exterior of the vehicle somewhat above 200 mrem/hour.

Radiation Limits for Exclusive Use Vehicles

Packages that exceed the radiation levels previously mentioned must be transported by exclusive use[2]. **Packages** in exclusive use vehicles may have radiation levels up to 1,000 mrem/hour on their exterior surface provided that:

a) the shipment is made in a Closed Transport Vehicle[3];

b) the package is secured within the vehicle so that its position remains fixed during transportation, and

c) there are no loading or unloading operations between the beginning and end of the transportation.

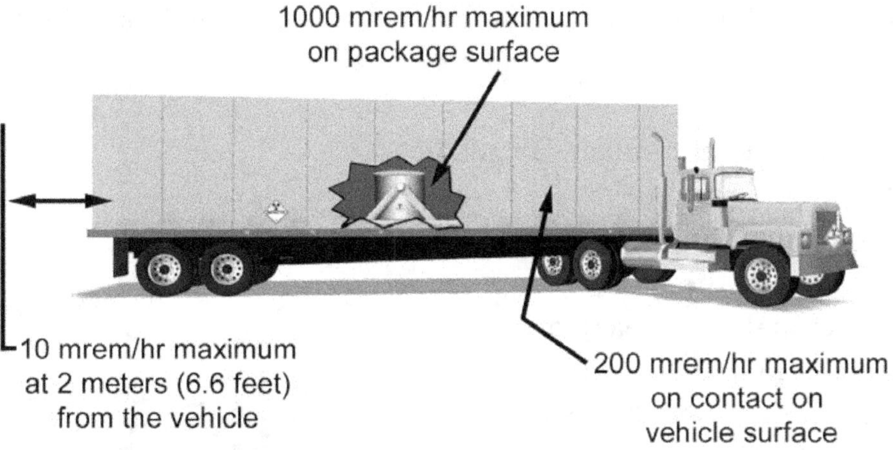

No point on the outer surfaces, or outer plane, of the vehicle may exceed 200 mrem/hour. Radiation levels at 2 meters from the vehicle cannot exceed 10 mrem/hour. Drivers of exclusive shipments are required to have specific written instructions for the shipment. These instructions must be included with the shipping papers.

Note: To determine if a shipment is being transported under the exclusive use provisions, you can look at the shipping papers, ask the driver, and/or contact the shipper.

---

[2] "Exclusive use" means a single shipper transports the material and all initial, intermediate, and final loading and unloading are carried out in accordance with the direction of the shipper or receiver.

[3] Closed Transport Vehicle means a transport vehicle or conveyance equipped with a securely attached exterior enclosure that, during normal transportation, restricts the access of unauthorized persons to the cargo space.

Checking Packages for External Contamination

If a package appears to be breached or you suspect it may be breached, you can check for the presence of removable contamination by taking a smear of the package. Removable contamination is defined as the radioactive material that can be transferred from a surface by rubbing with moderate pressure. The smear (or wipe/swipe test) is the universal method of assessing removable contamination. A small cloth, filter paper, or fiberglass disk is used to "wipe" an area or object suspected of being contaminated. A smear should cover a minimum surface area of 100 cm^2 (approximately equal to a square measuring 4" by 4"). Smears should be dry and taken using moderate pressure. Protective clothing should always be worn when taking smear samples to minimize the chance of personnel contamination.

Individual smear samples should be kept separate to avoid cross contamination. Smear packets (similar to the one pictured at right) make this easy and are available from a variety of vendors. If pieces of cloth or paper towel are used, they can

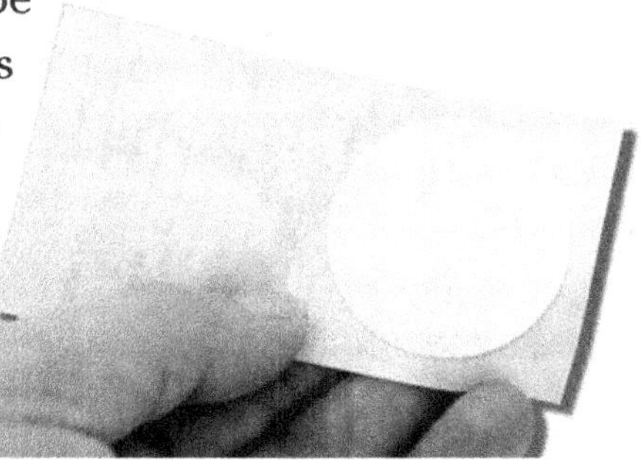

be kept separate by using plastic storage bags. Data should be maintained indicating the date and location of each smear sample.

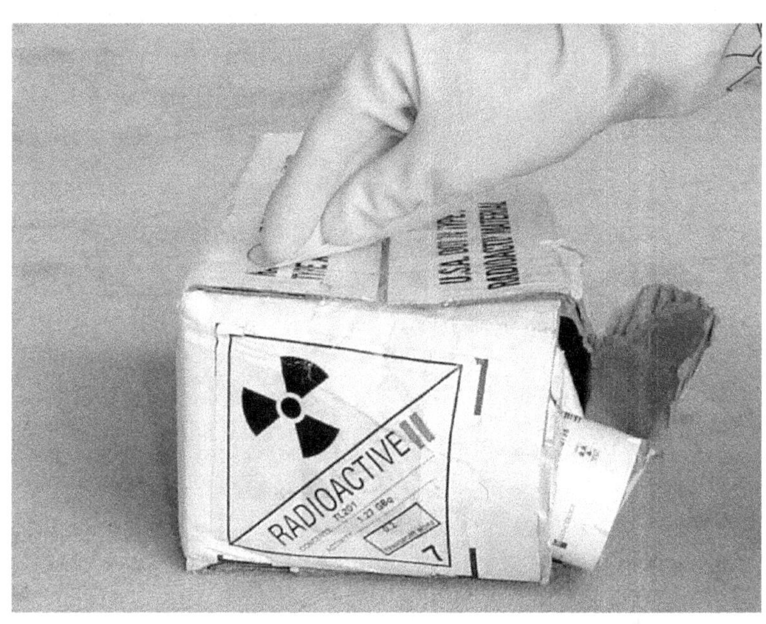

M E R R T T
Assessing Package Integrity

Smears can be counted (surveyed) in the field using a contamination survey meter. The smear(s) should be counted in a low background area by properly trained personnel. Count the smears by holding the probe approximately ½" from the surface of the smear. Pause for 5-10 seconds over the area to provide adequate time for instrument response. Become familiar with your jurisdiction's or state's guidelines for when an object is considered contaminated. For example, some jurisdictions use twice background or 100 CPM above background as a positive indication of contamination. Field counting techniques, like those described here, can be used to check for removable contamination, but may not be appropriate for releasing material as "clean." Release surveys should be conducted under the direction of the state or local Radiation Authority.

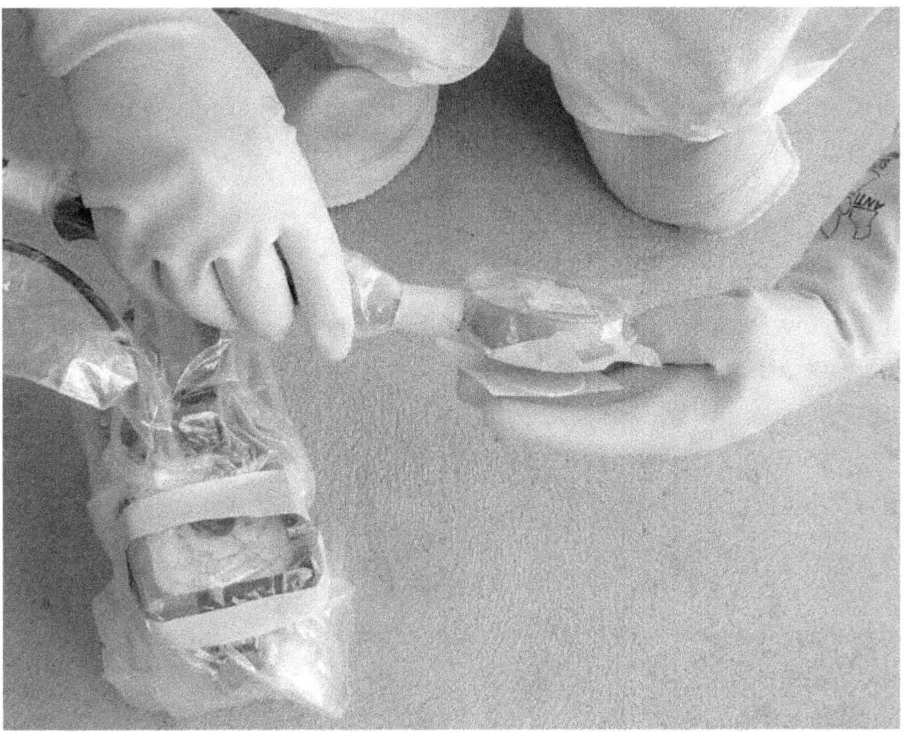

Check Your *Understanding*

1. An undamaged package with a Radioactive White-I label can have a maximum radiation level of _______ mrem/hour at the surface of the package.
   a) 50 mrem/hour
   b) 200 mrem/hour
   c) 0.5 mrem/hour
   d) 20 mrem/hour

2. How does the shipper obtain the transport index for a package?
   a) By taking the maximum radiation level (measured in mrem/hour) at one meter from the undamaged package.
   b) By taking the maximum weight of the package divided by the radiological dose rate.
   c) By taking the contact dose rate on the package's inner container.
   d) By taking the square root of the total number of packages allowed on the shipment.

3. The Radioactive __________ label is attached to packages with external radiation levels ranging from greater than 50 mrem/hour to a maximum of 200 mrem/hour.

4. The maximum radiation level on packages in non-exclusive use vehicles is _____ mrem/hour.

5. The maximum contact radiation level allowed on packages transported inside exclusive use closed transport vehicles is _____ mrem/hour.

M E R R T T

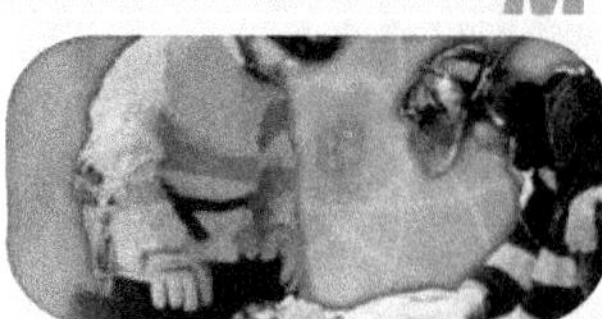 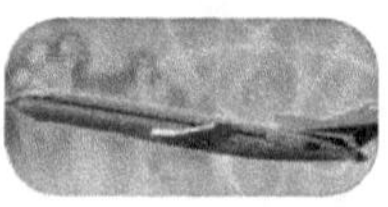  

M E R R T T
Decontamination, Disposal, & Documentation

notes

INTRODUCTION

This module discusses ways in which equipment and personnel can become contaminated with radioactive material and describes some field decontamination methods. Some of the PPE and equipment used in decontamination needs to be disposed of properly to prevent further spread of radioactive contamination. Once contaminated material is bagged, it needs to be clearly identified, documented, and disposed of properly.

PURPOSE

The purpose of this module is to inform you of methods used to decontaminate personnel and equipment. This information will help you prevent further spread of radiological contamination and minimize the amount of radioactive waste generated when performing response activities at the scene of a transportation incident involving radioactive material.

MODULE OBJECTIVES

Upon completion of this module, you will be able to:

1. Identify how personnel, personal protective equipment, apparatus, and tools become contaminated with radioactive material.
2. State the purpose of radioactive decontamination.
3. Identify field decontamination techniques for equipment.
4. Identify field decontamination techniques for personnel.
5. Identify your responsibilities for radioactive material disposal and event documentation.

RADIOACTIVE CONTAMINATION

Radioactive contamination is undesired radioactive material deposited on the surfaces of or inside structures, areas, objects, or people. Radioactive material can be solid, liquid, or gaseous. If radioactive material is released from a package, personnel, personal protective equipment (PPE), apparatus, and tools can become contaminated if they contact this material. When individuals (accident victims or response personnel), PPE, or equipment become contaminated, the contamination can easily be spread by cross-contamination or secondary contamination to other persons, equipment, or surfaces. Care should be taken to avoid cross-contamination. The following practices will help to avoid spreading contamination:

- Change gloves after handling accident victims and contaminated equipment
- Avoid unnecessary activity in the contaminated area
- Sleeve or wrap equipment prior to entry into the area
- Adhere to the policy of no eating, drinking, smoking, or chewing in the hot zone
- Avoid touching unprotected skin areas

Performing a thorough contamination survey on individuals and equipment exiting the hot zone can also help minimize the spread of contamination.

Personnel can become contaminated internally, externally, or both. Internal contamination occurs when radioactive material is ingested or inhaled or otherwise taken into the body. External contamination occurs when radioactive material gets on you or your clothing.

RADIOACTIVE DECONTAMINATION

Radioactive decontamination involves removing radioactive material (contamination) from locations where it is not wanted. Decontamination is performed in order to:

- Decrease radiation exposure by removing the radioactive material
- Prevent further spread of radioactive material
- Prevent or decrease the risk of internal contamination

FIELD DECONTAMINATION

Field decontamination means setting up a decontamination station near the incident scene and performing decontamination of personnel and equipment. If equipment is not to be decontaminated in the field, it will need to be bagged, clearly identified as "radioactive," and properly shipped to a facility where decontamination can be performed. When field decontamination procedures are being considered, evaluate the advantages and limitations of field decontamination.

Advantages

One of the main advantages of field decontamination is that it removes the source of contamination and limits the potential spread of contamination. Decontaminating equipment can free up potentially contaminated resources needed outside the hot zone.

Limitations

Field decontamination is time consuming. Untrained personnel can further slow the process. Even when personnel have been decontaminated, they cannot be considered "clean" until surveyed by a properly trained radiation authority.

A lack of properly trained personnel is the limiting factor. Personnel often lack training not only in radiological instrument use, but also in proper methods of field decontamination.

Another limitation of field decontamination is that using wet methods may produce large quantities of water or liquid that will need to be contained, surveyed, and properly disposed of if found to be contaminated.

M E R R T T
Decontamination, Disposal, & Documentation

FIELD DECONTAMINATION SET-UP

If field decontamination is necessary, it is important to establish a decontamination station/area. As with other hazardous material incidents, the decontamination corridor is usually established inside the warm zone running between the hot zone and cold zone. The Incident Commander and Safety Officer will determine where the decontamination corridor should be established and will consider the following:

- Wind direction relative to incident scene
- Background radiation levels
- Hot, warm, and cold zone boundaries
- Areas for best access into and out of incident scene

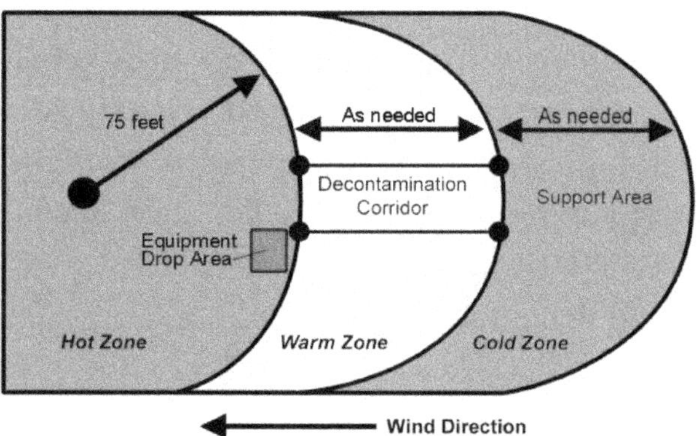

The decontamination corridor will need the following:

- **Equipment drop area** (inside hot zone) - This is where tools, equipment, etc., should be set down to wait for radiological survey. A small piece of plastic or poly can be placed on the ground to define the drop area. The plastic or poly will also serve to protect the ground from secondary contamination from equipment.

- **Clothing removal station** - This is where protective clothing will be removed and placed into appropriate containers (provide plastic lined containers).

- **Radiological survey station** - This is the area where, after removing protective clothing, personnel are surveyed for radiological contamination. Radiological surveys need to be performed by qualified individuals. Personnel who are contaminated must go to the decontamination station. Personnel who survey "clean" will be allowed to exit into the cold zone. If you suspect that personnel exiting the hot zone may not be contaminated, you may want to consider surveying them prior to removal of their protective clothing. If personnel survey clean while wearing their protective clothing, the clothing will not need to be disposed of as radioactive waste. Personnel should be surveyed again after removal of their protective clothing.

- **Decontamination station** - This is where personnel decontamination is performed. After decontamination, personnel will return to the radiological survey station for a second survey to determine the effectiveness of the decontamination effort.

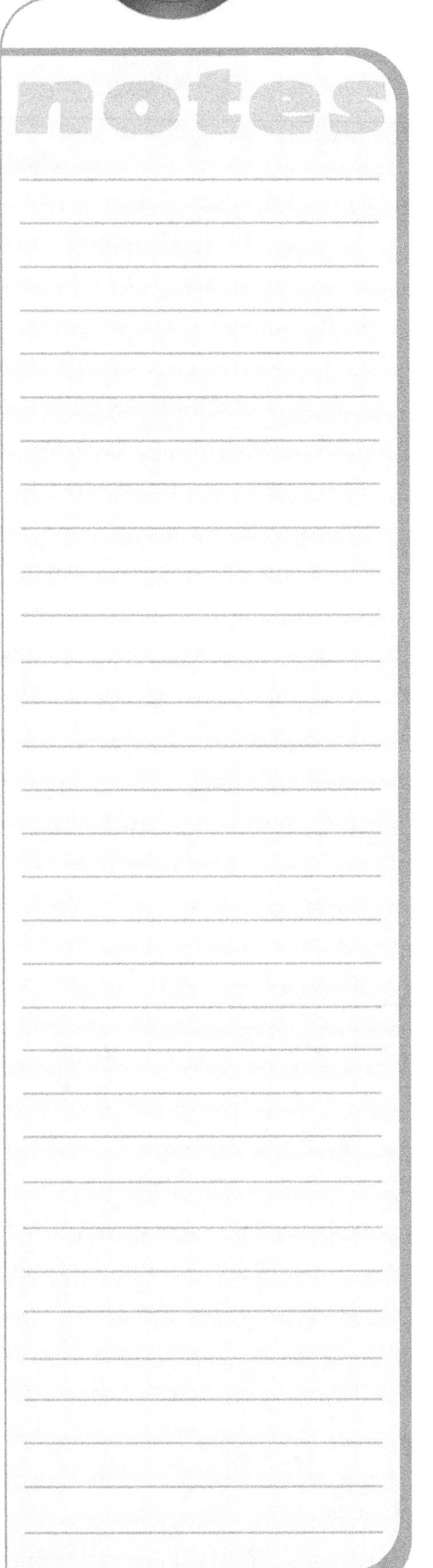

EQUIPMENT DECONTAMINATION

Equipment decontamination involves removing radiological contamination from equipment. Not all equipment can be decontaminated (e.g., straps, porous material, equipment with inaccessible areas). Some preplanning before taking material into the hot zone can help prevent equipment from becoming contaminated. For example, equipment can be placed in a clear poly bag before being taken into the contaminated area. Upon exit from the area, the contaminated bag can be removed and disposed of. Radiological Control personnel routinely bag radiological survey instruments prior to entering a contaminated area to prevent instruments from being contaminated.

If equipment needs to be decontaminated, consider the following methods:

- **Critical hand-held equipment** - Trained personnel can attempt to decontaminate equipment by wiping it down with a damp, absorbent cloth
- **Critical heavy equipment** - Trained personnel can attempt decontamination using a non-abrasive wash solution

All solid and liquid waste generated during decontamination will need to be controlled, properly packaged, and stored for eventual disposal in accordance with local procedures.

M E R R T T
Decontamination, Disposal, & Documentation

PERSONNEL DECONTAMINATION

Use of traditional hazardous material decon procedures may not be necessary if radioactive material is the only hazard present. While use of traditional hazardous material decon processes are effective for radioactive material, their use may generate large quantities of wastewater. Consideration should be given to methods that will minimize the amount of waste generated. There are simpler methods available for decon that are less time consuming, require fewer resources, and generate less waste.

Removing all clothing (gross decon) can dramatically reduce the contaminants on a person's body. After performing a gross decon, clothing should be left inside the hot zone. This clothing should be contained and controlled until surveyed. Minimizing the accumulation of contaminated or radioactive material (removed clothing, packages, etc.) in the area will help keep area radiation dose rates low. Localized areas of dry or loose contamination on clothing can be removed using a tape press. The method is similar to how lint would be removed from clothing.

Personnel decontamination of the skin may be accomplished by using conventional cleansing techniques on localized contaminated body surfaces (i.e., gentle washing and flushing that does not abrade the skin surface). When washing and flushing skin surfaces, mild soap and lukewarm water are preferred. Lukewarm water is preferred because cold water can cause skin pores to close, fixing the contamination into the skin. Hot water can cause skin pores to open, allowing the contamination to go deeper into the skin. Any water or material used in this process needs to be contained and considered radioactive waste. For localized contamination, pre-packaged pre-moistened wipes may be used instead of water to minimize the amount of waste generated. Techniques beyond gross decon should only be performed by properly trained personnel and under the direction of the Radiation Authority.

A model procedure showing methods for personnel decontamination is located in the appendix to this module and can be found on the MERRTT CD-ROM or on the TEPP website at http://www.energy.gov/em/services/waste-management/packaging-and-transportation/transportation-emergency-preparedness.

M E R R T T
Decontamination, Disposal, & Documentation

STOPPING FURTHER RELEASE OF RADIOACTIVE MATERIAL

Minimizing the spread of radioactive material is important during the emergency phase of an incident. This is usually the responsibility of the hazardous material response team. If you are not trained in methods for controlling the spread of radioactive material, DO NOT attempt them. Let properly trained personnel take this responsibility. Some things you can do are:

- Dike or contain any runoff water that may be contaminated
- Ensure that equipment inside the hot zone stays there until surveyed for contamination
- Ensure that all fires are out as soon as possible to limit the spread of radioactive material via smoke

WASTE DISPOSAL

Waste disposal can be a problem at any hazardous material scene. For a radiological incident, processes should be put in place as soon as possible to ensure all radioactive waste is contained.

1. Have plastic-lined waste containers at the entry/exit of the decontamination corridor for disposing of potentially contaminated material. These containers are often the same as for other hazardous material contaminated wastes.
2. Seal the tops of full plastic bags and place them in a holding area inside the hot zone. Ensure that containers are clearly identified as "radioactive" and are properly stored for disposal later.

3. Ensure that the area is monitored periodically because, as waste material accumulates, increased radiation dose rates are possible.

4. Let properly trained personnel (state response team, hazardous material response team, and contractors) survey waste material for contamination. Contaminated waste will need to be disposed of in accordance with applicable regulations.

5. Survey all personnel and equipment prior to their exit from the hot zone. Items found to be contaminated should be decontaminated or properly packaged for future decontamination or disposal.

Other Considerations

Prior to making decisions about disposing of any material as waste, or taking the time to decontaminate material and equipment, consider the following:

- Many radioactive materials have very short half-lives. Commonly shipped medical and research isotopes have half-lives of hours or days. Short-lived material can be sealed in a container to await decay of the material to a stable or non-radioactive state.

- When using large quantities of water for decontamination, remember that the water has to be handled as radioactive material. Contaminated water can be difficult to deal with and expensive to process.

- Do not generate unnecessary waste. Use only the material needed to complete a safe and effective response.

M E R R T T
Decontamination, Disposal, & Documentation

notes

DISPOSAL AND DOCUMENTATION RESPONSIBILITIES

Once the initial response phase of the incident is over, the focus will switch to cleanup and disposal of radioactive waste. The carrier is responsible for costs associated with scene cleanup and the disposal of radioactive material/waste. Carriers of radioactive material are required to provide financial protection to the public in the unlikely event of an incident involving radioactive material. The required amount of liability coverage for carriers of radioactive material varies according to the mode of transport (road, rail, waterway, or air) and the type and quantity of radioactive material being shipped. If the damages from a transportation-related accident (radiological) exceed the amount of the carrier's private insurance coverage, umbrella coverage is provided under the Price-Anderson Act.

Event documentation and reporting is an important step in recovering costs associated with a transportation incident involving hazardous material. Time, resources, and property damage must be recorded for payment. Documentation will be the legal evidence necessary in the future. Your documentation must include: who, what, when, where, how, and why.

DOE has a model Hazardous Materials Team Incident Response Procedure available that will assist in documenting response activities. The procedure can be found on the MERRTT CD-ROM or on the TEPP website at: http://www.energy.gov/em/services/waste-management/packaging-and-transportation/transportation-emergency-preparedness

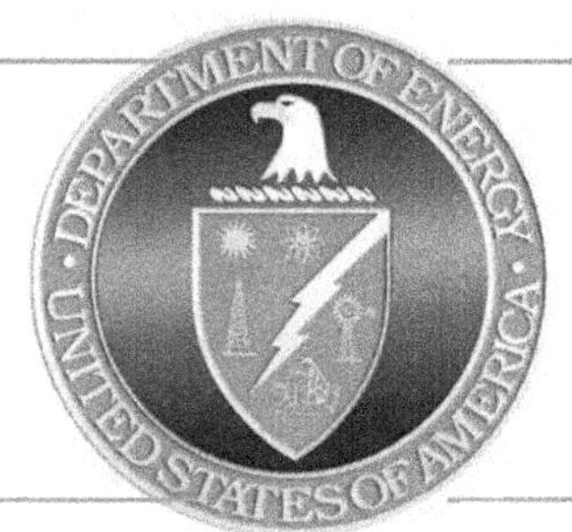

1. Radioactive material can take the form of a _____, _______, or ____.

2. List two reasons for performing radiological decontamination.

   ____

   ____

3. Personnel _____________ is usually accomplished using mild soap and lukewarm water.

4. Which of the following statements is true regarding equipment decontamination?
   a) Contaminated equipment should be hosed off immediately
   b) Contaminated equipment should not be taken into the hot zone
   c) Equipment that is contaminated should be disposed of as radioactive waste
   d) Not all equipment can be decontaminated

5. For decontamination operations, a _____________ ___________ is usually established inside the warm zone, running between the hot zone and cold zone.

6. The ________ is responsible for costs associated with scene cleanup and the disposal of radioactive material/waste.

7. Event _____________ and reporting is an important step in recovering costs associated with a transportation incident involving hazardous material.

ANSWERS

1. solid
   liquid
   gas
2. See page 3
3. decontamination
4. d
5. decontamination
   corridor
6. carrier
7. documentation